11070I672

Dreamscape

P®

WITHDRAWN

Cover Art by *MADHU*

Dreamscape
Voyage in an Alternate Reality

Bruce A. Vance

This publication is made possible with
the assistance of the Kern Foundation

The Theosophical Publishing House
Wheaton, Ill. U.S.A.
Madras, India/London, England

The Theosophical Publishing House
306 West Geneva Road
Wheaton, IL 60187

A publication of the Theosophical Publishing House, a
department of the Theosophical Society in America.

Library of Congress Cataloging-in-Publication Data

Vance, Bruce A., 1953-
    Dreamscape : voyage in an alternate reality / Bruce A.
Vance. — 1st ed.
        p.   cm.
    ISBN 0-8356-0648-1 : $8.95
    1. Dreams.   I. Title.
BF1078.V355   1989
135'.3—dc20   89-40176
                                                        CIP

Printed in the United States of America

With affection and gratitude for their unfailing support,
this book is dedicated to my parents,
Gene and Shirley Vance

Contents

Preface

The concept of an alternate, nonphysical reality into which individuals may venture is as old as humanity. The techniques which enable seekers to enter this realm differ from culture to culture and from age to age. In many cases only those with exceptional abilities—shamans, priests and priestesses, yogis, persons of power and knowledge—can approach this mysterious realm. I believe, however, that each of us has access to this alternate reality, but for the most part we have failed to see the door that stands open for us—perhaps because that door is so very close.

Journeying to the nonphysical realms has long been practiced among cultures in which shamanism has played a key part. In *Shamanism: Archaic Techniques of Ecstasy* Mircea Eliade thoroughly documented the shamanistic beliefs and practices of peoples in such wide-ranging cultures as Indonesia, Asia, the Arctic, and North America. Among the Turko-Tatars, the Siberian Tatars, the Eskimos, the Semang Pygmies, the Dusun of North Borneo, and dozens of other cultures, journeys to either the "Upper" or "Sky World" and to the "Lower" or "Under World" have been—and are today—an important part of life. Eliade was among the first to show us that in all cultures where shamanism exists, there is a strong belief in the existence of nonphysical realms.

More recently anthropologist Michael Harner, in

his book *The Way of the Shaman,* documented a belief in an "Upper World" and a "Lower World" among the Jivaro of the Ecuadoran Andes. The shamans of this culture travel these realms frequently. Carlos Castaneda has written eight books, beginning with *The Teachings of Don Juan: A Yaqui Way of Knowledge,* in which he describes his apprenticeship under a Yaqui Indian sorcerer, demonstrating that in Central America "nonordinary realities" are visited by those adept in the necessary techniques. And there is abundant evidence to show that the Aranda shamans of Australia, the Angakok of the Eskimos, and shamans of Japan all venture into the nonphysical realms.

The Senoi of Malaysia and the Iroquois of North America are among those who see the path of the dreamer as the one most suited for entering and exploring the nonphysical realm. They believe that the inner life we encounter in dreams is at least as real as, if not more real than the life we experience in the waking world. The Washo tribes of California and Nevada believe that through dreams we may hold communion with natural and supernatural spirits.

Nearly every religion has some concept of a nonphysical reality. In Hinduism there are many levels to the nonphysical dimension. The visions of saints and mystics occur beyond the limits of ordinary human perception. Descents into the Under World and ascents into the Upper World by religious figures have been recorded in the literature of Christianity and Buddhism. Whether through shamanic journeys, ecstatic visions, altered states of consciousness, or dream journeys, travels into a nonphysical dimension have been an integral part of humanity's search for understanding and expansion since the human species began to roam the earth.

Today there is a resurgence of interest in this age-old quest which compels men and women everywhere to seek a pathway into an alternate reality, a reality out of which our greatest myths are born, a reality out of which, perhaps, our very lives unfold. In an age of technology once again we are seeking routes into a dimension where the greatest scientific achievements are transcended by the mechanisms of reality itself.

Entering the nonphysical dimension can require years of preliminary training or the guidance of a teacher who is versed in esoteric techniques according to some discipline. However, each of us ventures into an alternate reality every night, treading a pathway into the nonphysical dimension. This is the path of the dreamer.

I began recalling my dreams when I was five or six years old. Sometimes they frightened me, sometimes they thrilled me, but they never bored me. I soon found that I could influence my dreams by telling myself before I went to sleep what I wanted to dream about, horses, for example; I subsequently did so. Upon waking from a particularly pleasant dream I learned that with effort I could reenter it, continuing from where I had left off. The dreams of my childhood were often mysterious, even bizarre, and because they influenced me so much I could not dismiss them as meaningless. At the very least they had an effect upon both my emotional and mental states during my waking hours. How could something so real, I asked myself, be unimportant?

Later in life I encountered many dream dictionaries which purported to give meanings for dream symbols. Supposedly, by looking up an image I had encountered while dreaming and reading the interpretation of it in one of these dictionaries, I could understand my dreams. What I found in those books was interesting and gave me food for thought, but didn't seem to get to the heart of the matter. I never got that inner "click" to indicate that I had solved the mystery.

I soon determined that such parlor-game approaches to interpreting the complexities and mysteries of dreaming were essentially meaningless. Individuals are unique, and their relationships to the facets of reality they encounter are equally unique. The experiences, attitudes, beliefs, and history of each individual influence how he or she will react or relate to any event, image, or symbol. What symbolizes freedom to one person may symbolize bondage to another. And so I quickly abandoned the dream dictionaries.

Any approach to the interpretation of dreams and the dream environment that fails to take into account the uniqueness of the individual is flawed. No one else can tell you what something means to you; no one can tell you why you have the experiences you do. Even if someone else could adequately interpret your experiences for you, or mine for me, it is only reasonable to assume that we will gain more through making our own discoveries.

The psychological approach to the study of dreams reinforced my early belief in the importance of dreaming experiences. Freud, Jung, and their followers declared that dreams are inextricably linked with the individual's psyche and are capable of producing important insights. These analysts and psychiatrists claimed that the elements of dreams are often portrayals of facets of the individual's personality. This psychological research stimulated me to investigate my own dreams further, and it helped me unravel some of the mysteries encountered therein. But something was still missing. I had too many dreaming experiences which could not be interpreted adequately as expressions of my own personality. The psychological approach did not explain these.

At last I realized that the only way I would ever discover the truth about dreams and dreaming was to make a thorough, direct investigation on my own, so I embarked upon a journey which lasted many years. I recorded all my dreams and applied myself to the task of unraveling their mysteries. I studied the works of other dreamers and other explorers of the nonphysical dimension; I applied their methods and tested their theories, and I created my own methods and tested my own theories. As a result, I soon discovered that there was no substitute for personal experience. This book, then, is the product of years of personal experience, containing the heart of what I have gleaned from the wonders I have encountered.

When evaluated in the light of our conceptions about the nature of reality as it is experienced in the physical dimension, dreams are confusing and highly enigmatic. During my years of exploring and studying this alternate reality I learned that the environment in which dreams occur is ordered much differently from physical reality. To understand dreams requires an understanding of the reality in which they occur: we will never unravel the mysteries of our dreams so long as we expect them to conform to the rules of the environment in which we spend our waking hours.

Reality has many faces. In the physical environment there is the *objective reality* about which we all can agree and which is conveyed to us through our physical senses, and there is the *subjective reality* which shows a different face to each individual. The subjective factor is determined by our thoughts, beliefs, attitudes, and desires. It determines whether

you will see a cloudy day as depressing or pleasant.
And it determines what you call good and what you
call bad. The subjective reality is cast like a film over
the objective reality, making each individual's relationship to reality unique.

In this respect I have found that the environment
of dreams is similar to the physical environment.
There is an objective dream environment, whose aspects and regions appear pretty much the same to all
who witness them. There are places which do not
change, no matter how many times you go there, and
there are forces which do not alter their natures according to the whims of the individual. But the subjective factor also enters into your experience of the
environment of dreams. In this alternate reality the
subjective factor plays an even more important part
than it does in the physical environment. I call this
realm of dreams the Dreamscape.

In some regions of the Dreamscape subjectivity is
the determining factor in all that is experienced.
Whereas in physical reality our inner states, concepts, and attitudes color our view of the objective
reality, in the environment of dreams subjectivity can
totally create the images we see and the events we
experience. There we create all that we experience,
and there is little or no agreement about what is perceived by those who journey to these realms.

The nonphysical reality of the dreamer has a "geography" that is closely allied to the factors of subjectivity and objectivity. The most subjective are
regions we most often recall; they are the ones that
shape themselves according to our thoughts, beliefs,
and desires. As we venture more deeply into this dimension subjectivity plays less of a role and we begin
to encounter levels of experience where things do not
change to accommodate our individual wishes. In

these planes we are no longer confronting our own projected natures, but instead are encountering the inhabitants of a nonphysical realm with its own inherent "geography."

This realm is independent of the parameters of space and time, so it is difficult for me to convey to you the nature of the geography of the dream environment. The various regions of the Dreamscape do not have a spatial relationship one to another as do the territories of physical reality. More often than not the inner state of the dreamer determines the relative proximity of locations. I can speak of different "planes," different "realms," or different "places," but unless you go there yourself such terms will make little sense. Suffice it to say that the Dreamscape is as varied as the physical world and each part of it is filled with wonders. Journeying to the different levels of the dream world requires a corresponding journey of consciousness, and I suspect that there are many areas of the Dreamscape which we will never see so long as our primary focus of consciousness is in the physical realm.

Our consciousness is our awareness as it exists independently of the tools of perception we employ in any particular dimension. When our consciousness is focused in physical reality, the physical senses are the tools of perception; in other realms finer senses come into play. As you journey through the Dreamscape your consciousness will shift focus; it will engage nonphysical senses and will adopt forms other than those with which you now identify. If you wish to explore this alternate reality thoroughly, you will have to free yourself of limiting concepts of identity, trusting that your consciousness, your overriding awareness, is forever inviolable.

In this book I hope to share with you my own discoveries regarding the nature of this alternate reality. I hope to provide an approach to the interpretation of dreams which will enable you to uncover the meanings behind your own dream experiences. And I hope to encourage you to undertake a serious and prolonged exploration of this dimension in which dreaming takes place.

You will find no interpretations of individual dreams in this book. No specific meanings for symbols and images will be detailed. Unraveling the mysteries of dreaming is no easy matter, and I will not pretend that things are otherwise. Hopefully, you are reading this book because you are serious about investigating the nature of your dreaming experiences and the environment in which dreams take place. If you are, then I believe this book will be of help to you.

Experience has convinced me that studying dreams can be tremendously valuable and rewarding, and that there is much to learn. We are at a stage in human development where many people are attempting to transcend the current limits of our understanding of the immense reality which envelops us, by investigating consciousness and its relationships to reality. Our dreams have always been with us, beckoning us to investigate the mysteries they convey. If we truly seek self-knowledge we cannot afford to dismiss any experiences, including those we encounter while our bodies sleep.

I am convinced that dreaming involves us in far more than simple ramblings inspired by the events of our daily lives and our own psyches. While dreaming, we explore both the nature of reality and the nature of consciousness. We delve into the various levels of our own being and we venture into realms so different from the one in which we usually find ourselves, that from a purely physical perspective they are unimaginable. While dreaming, we make many determinations about the courses we will pursue in our daily lives. By subtly altering our dreaming focus of consciousness, we can train ourselves to be more alert to these activities as they are occurring.

I promise that if you persevere in your explorations of the dream environment and in your interpretations of your own dreams you will encounter much that is both illuminating and fascinating. Few people even imagine the wealth of information that is available to the dreamer, simply because they are convinced there is nothing to be found. If you are reading this book, then you are already a step ahead, because something within you is telling you that you will benefit from an investigation of your dreams.

I do not pretend to know all there is to know about dreaming, just as I do not profess to know all there is to know about life in the physical environment. But through years of intensive study of my own dream experiences I have learned enough so that my dreams are no longer confusing and unexplainable. There is a cohesiveness and a continuity to our experiences in the dream environment. There is meaning to everything that we experience there. And there is no end to how far we can travel into the mysteries of this alternate reality.

While dreaming we are freed from many of the restrictions which limit us in our waking reality. Time and space loosen their strict hold. Consciousness is allowed to change its focus and to perceive reality in new ways. The unfettered self can express more of its full nature.

We are far more than what we seem to be in physical reality. Through a serious investigation of all our experiences we can come to know and express more of what we truly are. Therefore, our experiences in the Dreamscape deserve our attention.

So there is a new frontier waiting for you to explore, vistas of unimaginable wonder waiting to be pioneered. In over ten years of exploration I have only glimpsed a small portion of this fantastic realm, and it is my hope that others will join me so that in collaboration we can begin to establish a more accurate map. The little I have seen is enough to compel me to share what I have found and to encourage others to venture on an exciting expedition into this frontier, the vastness of which eclipses any earthly region.

The laws which govern this strange territory are unlike any we have known before, but that is always the case when we venture into the unknown. I will not hide the truth and say that there is nothing to fear. Fear, however, is of our own making, and if you carry fear with you into this realm then you will encounter it there, because you must inevitably face yourself. At the same time there are marvelous opportunities, excitement, adventure, and discovery. This region of which I speak is not empty, desolate, and uninhabited; it is filled with life and energy and purpose.

If you choose to explore this new frontier with me you will not only discover its inherent wonders, but you also will gain invaluable insights into your own nature. This is a realm which invites total self-expression, a realm so fertile that the slightest thought can give rise to empires. Here you will discover your own vast powers of creativity, but you also will come face to face with your weaknesses and your self-created limitations.

Clearly, many people throughout history have given credence to the notion that dreams are not hallucinations but real, and that they hold something valuable for us. But has anyone told you of the grand territory in which you experience your dreams? I tell you that there is such a place; I have been there many times, and so have you. And I heartily invite you to explore with me this beckoning frontier.

Part 1

1

A New Frontier:
The Realm of Dreaming

People have consulted dreams for a long time and for a wide variety of reasons. Some have sought glimpses into the future; others the insights dreams can afford into times of crisis and into situations calling for important decisions. We can only speculate as to how important dreams may have been to early humans, lacking as they did other means of delving into the mysteries of existence.

The Bible tells of the Pharoah of Egypt placing great value on Joseph's ability to interpret dreams. In the ancient literature of the Buddhists and Tibetans numerous references are made to the valuable information that may be gained through the study of one's dreams. Historically, the Tibetans have looked to dreams to identify and locate each new incarnation of the Dalai Lama. In every community in every age there have been individuals who consulted their dreams in an attempt to further their understanding of the nature of reality.

In respect of the age-old search for greater understanding we are no different from our ancestors. We search for truth and insight wherever we believe they may be found. Since dreams, whatever their nature,

3

make up a part of everyone's experience, is it any wonder that we too, like our ancestors, are often compelled to probe the content of our nightly journeys for whatever insights they may afford? We intuitively know that there is a purpose to our dream lives, just as there is a purpose to our waking lives. Therefore we expand our search for truth into the realm of dreaming, into a frontier both new and old.

PAST RESEARCH AND PREVAILING ATTITUDES

Most Westerners' conceptions about dreams and dreaming draw upon a tradition of investigation which began with Austrian psychoanalyst Sigmund Freud. Though dreams have excited interest since the dawn of humanity, it was not until Freud did his pioneering work in the area of psychology during the early part of this century that serious interest in dreams was renewed in Western civilization. Since then attitudes towards the nature of dreams and their relative importance have undergone a multitude of changes. And since we have all been influenced to one degree or another by these changing attitudes, it is useful to briefly summarize their course.

Freud, in *The Interpretation of Dreams*, wrote of his belief that dreams essentially express our irrational sides. According to him, symbolic forms are the language of dreams, and are difficult to interpret precisely because they are intended to cloak the unpleasantries they express. He felt that dreams served as a "safety valve," enabling the dreamer to act out fantasies and repressed wishes. Their symbolic nature serves as a guardian of sleep by preventing unpleasant fantasies from intruding on our conscious minds and disturbing us while we rest. Freud interpreted dreams from a causal point of view, assuming that they are the result of unfulfilled wishes from the previous day, wishes caused by childhood fantasies, fears, and desires.

Carl Jung, Freud's pupil, believed that Freud's theory of dreams is too limiting. Though he agreed that some aspects of dreams are caused by unfulfilled wishes, he also thought that dreams often give us glimpses into the future, that they involve a psychological striving for a goal. He saw that dreams frequently outline solutions to problems or conflicts. Jung further surmised that all dreams serve a compensatory function: they involve the self-regulation of the psychic organism by balancing our conscious attitudes and beliefs with unconscious dream-dramas.

Jung believed that all figures within one's dreams are personified aspects of one's own personality. However, at the same time he felt that these utterances of the unconscious may involve revelations of wisdom which go beyond the conscious awareness of the individual. They contain not only fantasies and repressed wishes, but also deep truths, plans for the future, philosophical pronouncements, and even telepathic visions. So Jung led the psychological community to consider that dreams might have a far greater purpose than that outlined by Freud. He expressed these views in his book *Dreams* and in various scientific journals.

Outside of the established scientific community other individuals were pursuing their own lines of investigation into the nature of dreams. Edgar Cayce, the American psychic often called "The Sleeping Prophet," was one of these. Cayce, like Jung, believed that all aspects of our nature are revealed in dreams and that dreams lead us toward a greater, overall balance in our lives. According to Harmon H. Bro in *Edgar Cayce on Dreams*, Cayce felt that dreams are

meant to accomplish two things: to help solve the
problems of an individual's waking life, and to awaken
and bring to the surface new potentialities and abilities for the dreamer to claim.

According to Cayce, dreams not only serve as the
basis for self-analysis; they also contain ESP (extra-
sensory perception), glimpses into past lives, and
mystical experiences of the divine. He felt that every
dreamer has a repertoire of personal symbols and that
the individual, therefore, is best qualified to interpret
his or her own dreams. Though the scientific community was by no means prepared to accept such
"radical" extensions of the theory of dreaming, Cayce
and other investigators such as Ouspensky helped to
expand the frontiers of dream research.

In the second half of this century various professionals and laypersons have helped to further research into the nature of dreaming. Most have
essentially accepted Jung's concepts but expanded
upon them. In her book *Dreams, Your Magic Mirror*
Elsie Sechrist suggests four sources of dreams: one's
own subconscious, the subconscious of another person with whom the dreamer may be in contact, one's
superconscious, and God. She believes that dreams
are of four basic types: physical, mental, emotional,
and spiritual. Like Jung, she believes that we essentially meet ourselves in our dreams in any number of
clever disguises.

Erich Fromm also believed that sleep involves self-
experience, and that dreams are purely mental activities, as he indicated in *The Forgotten Language*. His
work essentially has involved an exploration into the
nature of symbols. Frederick Perls is another who felt
that dreams are a part of the dreamer's own personality, as demonstrated in *Gestalt Therapy Verbatim*,
and that dream images represent alienated elements

of the personality which we have pushed away because we are unable to accept them.

In the 1970s Ann Faraday wrote two books based on her research into dreaming. These, *Dream Power* and *The Dream Game*, have helped many people come to a greater understanding of their own dreams. Following the lead of Jung and Perls, Faraday believes that the dreaming process is always tied to the individual's present life and concerns. She contends that dreams can be understood on many different levels, but the basic purpose of all dreams is to give us insights into our daily lives. Faraday doubts that any information processing actually occurs within the dream state.

These are but a few of the individuals who have contributed to our limited understanding of dreams and dreaming. Others, like Celia Green, Oliver Fox, and Stephen LaBerge, have concentrated their explorations on *lucid dreams* in which the dreamer knows that he or she is dreaming. None of these people, however, has written about the possibility that the environment in which dreams take place has an objective reality. Nor has any of them taken into account the multidimensional nature of the self, or the likelihood that we have multidimensional experiences.

Though these researchers have contributed immeasurably to the study and understanding of dreams we must guard against basing our own beliefs and attitudes about dreaming on the beliefs and attitudes of others. There is much to be gained from studying their work and applying their techniques, but we cannot limit ourselves to the findings of the past. Every level of understanding can be transcended by a wider view.

Our attitudes toward our inner selves are influenced by our cultural belief systems; these have a bearing on our attitudes toward dreaming. Certain traditional religious, psychological, and scientific doctrines depict the inner world of the self as evil, confused, or uncontrollable. Such views hinder or limit our ability to understand the realities of the inner life. Whether we fully agree with such views or not, most of us unconsciously have picked up some of these attitudes. Before exploring your dream life, it is advisable to examine what you believe about the nature of your inner self, where these beliefs came from, and whether they will limit and color your understanding of the workings of your consciousness and the realms in which it moves.

Fortunately, a new light is beginning to break forth, if faintly, within the scientific, religious, and medical communities. More and more professionals are willing to recognize their own limitations in the area of dreams, and welcome the pursuits and findings of the individual. Psychologists are beginning to see that ultimately the individual must unravel the complexities of his or her own inner nature. Many doctors recognize that people have remarkable capacities for self-healing. More and more religious authorities recognize that the individual may meet with God anywhere, without the intercession of a church official. This is an age of independence. Individuals everywhere are beginning to take responsibility for their own relationships with reality. The Protestant movement began the process of wresting authority from the Church by proclaiming that the individual can have a direct relationship with God. Democracy has ousted kings and proclaimed that citizens can govern themselves, accepting responsibility for their mistakes as well as their accomplishments. In recent years untold numbers have taken up the challenge of self-analysis, self-exploration, and self-discovery, unrestrained by the dictates of self-proclaimed authorities.

If you would embark on an expedition into the mysterious Dreamscape in the spirit of finding out for yourself, if you seek to find its meanings and purposes, you must be prepared to rely upon your own counsel. You must be prepared to chart your own course through the immense mystery that is your self. The Dreamscape is, for the most part, unexplored and unexplained because we have believed that it is only subjective, at most an expression of the unconscious, and that we can do no more than hope to glean some meaning from its utterances. Fortunately, there are always some individuals who are willing to trust in themselves and go where others have feared to go. I hope you are one of them.

THE OBJECTIVE REALITY OF THE DREAMER'S ENVIRONMENT

In recent years scientists have come to realize that the physical world, as solid as it seems, is composed, in fact, of energy. Objects are composed of molecules, molecules of atoms, atoms of subatomic particles, and subatomic particles of quanta of energy. The appearance of solidity arises when one object is unable to pass through another, when the energy matrix of one object will not penetrate the energy matrix of another. However, when we take a subatomic particle and fire it at a table, it easily passes through. What has happened to the solidity of the table? The solidity of physical objects is an illusion.

It should be clear to anyone who is even vaguely familiar with the current findings of science that we live in a world composed of energy. We can perceive only that portion of the physical world our physical senses register. Our range of perception is limited and our senses cannot perceive energy levels which fall outside the range of the physical world. Even in the physical world there are forms and varieties of energy—such as x-rays, radio waves, and ultraviolet rays—that we cannot perceive without the aid of sophisticated scientific instruments.

The Dreamscape, the environment in which dreams take place, is also composed of energy; but it is energy of a different order from that which we are able to measure physically. The Dreamscape is composed of energy which falls outside the range of our most sophisticated scientific instruments and cannot be known through the physical senses. Yet it is a viable, existent reality nonetheless.

In more recent times nonphysical realities have been referred to extensively by writers such as Michael Harner, Carlos Castaneda, Mircea Eliade, and others who have studied shamanistic traditions. But the shamans are not the only ones to venture beyond the limits of the physical world. C. W. Leadbeater and Annie Besant wrote many books detailing their encounters with a nonphysical dimension. They discuss the *astral* and *etheric* bodies, nonphysical counterparts to our physical bodies which cannot be perceived through the ordinary physical senses but which nevertheless generate and interact with thought forms. (I cover this subject in more detail in Chapter Eight.) Jane Roberts, a writer, was channel for an entity known as Seth who discussed different levels of the "Unknown Reality" which exist in a nonphysical state. The religious and mystical literature of the Hindus and the Tibetans abound with references to nonphysical realms. The Senoi dreamers of Malaysia, whom I talk about later in this book, have long considered the environment of dreams to be a real place, open to exploration and filled with wonders. So have the Native Americans.

I could go on and on citing references such as these, for nearly every culture in every age has produced individuals who have experienced this nonphysical realm and described it within the context of that age and culture. At the same time, most so-called civilized cultures have produced individuals who have flatly denied the existence of any such realm.

As always, individuals must find the truth of the matter for themselves. I believe that, just as we are equipped with senses that enable us to perceive the physical world, so are we equipped with senses that enable us to perceive the dream environment, the realm of nonphysical reality. When you dream you actually see what is before you, you hear the real communications of others. You also perceive the dream environment in a number of other ways. Perhaps our thoughts are the simplest analogy to some of our perceptions in the Dreamscape. You "hear" your own thoughts, you "see" the images you form in your mind. Does the fact that you cannot physically see or hear your own thoughts make them any less real?

The environment of dreams does not exist some "where" else. It exists here and now, at a level and frequency of energy that is too subtle and too accelerated to be perceived by the physical senses. Perceiving it requires the use of more subtle and more accelerated senses. For the most part, when we are involved with our daily, physical lives we are too overwhelmed by the energies of this environment to perceive the subtle reality of the Dreamscape. However, some individuals are able to attune their consciousnesses to their subtle senses so that even while awake they perceive aspects of the environment most of us only experience when we sleep. Auras, visions, and images perceived under the influence of strong hallucinogenics are but a few examples of the occasional encounters with this subtle reality by individuals who are immersed in the physical world.

When you sleep, your conscious attention is free of

its fixation on the energy which composes our physical world. The distractions of the powerful energies of this world are removed, as are many of the inhibiting attitudes which limit your perceptual abilities. While your physical body and sensory organs sleep, your conscious awareness remains awake. At these times your focus is turned in another direction—toward the environment of dreams.

The Dreamscape is, in my opinion, quite real; it has an objectively valid reality. We can and do perceive it. Our experiences within it have an effect upon us. There is as much to discover within it as there is within the physical environment—if not more. I cannot prove that the Dreamscape is real, anymore than scientists can prove that the physical world is real. Reality is a matter of definition. If reality consists of that which we can perceive with our physical senses, then the Dreamscape is not real, nor is God real, nor are thoughts and feelings. But if reality consists of all we can or do perceive, all that has an effect upon us, all that is a part of our experience of the infinity that is the All, then the Dreamscape is certainly as real as the physical environment.

Many of us may have trouble accepting the objective reality of the dream environment because of the immense subjective freedom which is possible within that realm. One level of the Dreamscape—the one with which we are most familiar as a result of remembering our dreams—allows us total freedom to create whatever we wish. Due to the less rigid nature of its energy structure and other of its inherent characteristics, the dream environment changes shape according to the will and imagination of the individual, at least at this level. If a person experiences no other aspect of the Dreamscape than this, it is easy to see how he or she would infer that the Dreamscape is a purely subjective phenomenon.

Take a moment, though, and consider another situation. Suppose you were in a small valley where your view was limited to your immediate surroundings. Given time, you could cut down every tree, build any structure you wanted, reshape the land; in fact, you could totally restructure your immediate environment to appear any way you wanted. Would this then make your little valley a purely subjective phenomenon simply because you were free to shape it as you chose?

The significant difference between this physical scenario and the situations you encounter in this familiar realm of the Dreamscape is that the reshaping of your immediate dream environment takes essentially no time. Time is very different in the Dreamscape, a subject I discuss later, and it is far more plastic than it is in physical reality.

In deeper recesses of the Dreamscape the reshaping of the environment is a joint project: others participate in the formation of the perceived reality. This can be likened to the creation of a city environment in which all the inhabitants participate. In yet other dimensions the dream environment does not change according to the will of the individual traveler; it remains relatively fixed, according to its own laws, to be perceived as it is by the dreamer.

Later I discuss some of the other features of the Dreamscape. But when exploring any new frontier those regions which are closest to our home territory must necessarily be encountered first. In the Dreamscape the earliest encountered dimension is the one where our private dreams and dream creations unfold. Though it may seem here that everything appears totally subjective, you must remember that we are dealing with an objective reality which, by its very nature, allows a great freedom of subjective expression. To ignore the objective reality of the

Dreamscape is to ignore its inviolable laws, and to ignore the laws of any realm is to limit understanding and freedom.

PREPARING FOR THE JOURNEY

It cannot be stated too often that what you put into something determines what you get out of it. This axiom holds true when it comes to exploring the Dreamscape and studying your dreams. If you make only a casual attempt to understand your dreams or venture half-heartedly into the environment where dreaming takes place, you will reap only a slight reward at most. At worst, you will encounter only the easily confusing nature of your dreams and probably will strike upon misleading interpretations. There are many ingrained attitudes which keep us from recalling our dreams and dreaming experiences, and continued effort is necessary in order to shift the weight of personal and societal attitudes in the direction of confidence and effectiveness.

Patience is essential. The import of many dreaming experiences, especially at first, will become clear only over the course of time. For example, precognitive dreams often cannot be seen for what they are until their predictive elements are manifested in physical reality. And the significance of many other experiences in the dream environment will not become evident until they can be viewed in the context of time, and in relationship to other events and aspects of life.

Some courage is needed, too. Deeper explorations of the Dreamscape inevitably will lead you to face elements of your psyche that have remained hidden up until now for various reasons, including fear and denial. In addition, the Dreamscape is necessarily foreign; thus, many unexpected and often unimaginable events and scenarios will transpire, even some which will shake your concept of identity.

But what is an adventure if it lacks the unexpected? The human psyche is a marvelous construct. It automatically hides anything that could be truly harmful—if such a thing exists at all—and keeps it hidden until you are prepared to deal with it. Other aspects of your self, however, know better than your conscious mind what you can truly handle. Don't assume that hidden material must remain so; if something can be discovered or encountered it is because you are ready to see it.

Finally, there is yet one more important trait to cultivate and maintain if you are to see into the truth of things: honesty. Being honest with yourself is paramount. If you come upon something you do not understand, admit that you are in the dark. To slap the easiest and most available explanation onto something foreign is to deny yourself the opportunity of ever really understanding it. Likewise, if or when your intuition tells you something you would rather not hear, you must be honest enough with yourself to face the truth. Ignoring or denying something keeps you from progressing further in your explorations. Strict honesty with yourself, coupled with humility and self-trust, will carry you through any adversity.

Don't expect to understand the Dreamscape completely in a week or in a year, just as you would not be able to understand the waking environment in so short a time. It often takes whole lifetimes to comprehend our destinies; it is likely to take just as long to come to a deep understanding and appreciation of the dream environment. Understanding comes gradually, each step building upon the previous one. So we must be committed to our search if we truly want to pioneer this strange realm. I am not saying that a casual or occasional exploration of dreams and the dream environment will reap no benefits, but to participate in the true wonders of dreaming requires sustained effort.

Anyone who has seriously sought self-knowledge realizes that the path is endless. Each level of understanding we reach must one day be transcended by a more encompassing view. We gain knowledge when we are ready for it, when we have laid the necessary foundation.

A sustained exploration of the Dreamscape will unfold aspects of reality to you which were previously unimagined. If you have not made a thorough study of your dreams, you may suspect that they always will appear distorted, disjointed, and at best capable of yielding but a few intriguing insights. If you venture far enough, however, you will be truly amazed at what can be found. And you will be amazed to discover where you can go and what you can accomplish within and through the Dreamscape.

Inevitably, through the study of dreams and the dream environment you also will achieve a greater understanding of waking reality. I believe that, from the broader viewpoint of the whole self, the waking environment is equivalent to one long dream from which we awaken at the point of death.

As I have said before, I believe that the experiences we have within the Dreamscape are every bit as real as those we have in the physical environment. In time you may come to find that they are even more real. So is imagination real, and so are daydreams. Don't make the mistake, however, of believing that their reality is structured according to the rules and laws of waking reality. When we try to interpret our experiences in the dream environment in terms of the rules of everyday physical reality we close ourselves off to their true reality.

Not all dreams are linked directly to occurrences within our daily lives. We do ourselves a grave injustice when we contend that our consciousness is bound to one dimension, when in fact we are multidimensional beings with our "psychic fingers" reaching throughout the universe.

It is tempting to categorize dreams, but the problem with doing this is that most if not all dreams partake of more than one aspect of existence. A dream experience may contain precognitive elements for example, and therapeutic healing aspects at the same time. Just as an event in physical reality may affect us emotionally as well as mentally, so do dream experiences affect us in multiple ways. To categorize a dream would be to limit its possible scope unnecessarily.

Some of the aspects of the dreaming experience that I will cover in this volume include: connections with daily events, precognition, attempts at choosing possible courses of action that are most suited to your purposes, the study and assessment of problems in your life, lucid dreams (in which you know you are in the Dreamscape), experiences relating to past and future lives, social interaction, unfoldings of the nature of the self, exercises in the art of creating your own reality, out-of-body experiences initiated from within the dream environment, "classroom" or learning situations, and, of course, forays into dimensions of reality in which the order of things is as alien to the common dream experience as the common dream experience is alien to waking reality.

It is necessary to learn to recognize and differentiate between the various aspects in our dreaming experiences if we are to arrive at fair and accurate interpretations. To interpret an out-of-body experience in the light of something which happened on a previous day, for example, would only lead to further

obscurity and misunderstanding. Truly, the Dreamscape is complex, but then so are we.

Before I go into the particulars of dream experiences it is important to examine some aspects of the
nature of reality in general and some aspects of the
Dreamscape in particular. Various concepts will be
put forth in this book which on first reading or taken
out of context may seem incredible at the very least.
I can only ask that you bear with me and appeal to
your own inner guidance to determine whether what
you read does or does not correspond with your inner
sense of truth. Each of us has a standard of truth
which invariably is, and must be, our guide into the
mysteries of existence. Simply because something
seems at first to be unbelievable is no reason to reject
it out of hand. If someone had told our ancestors that
some day human beings would walk on the moon,
how many of them would have laughed at such a
notion?

The Dreamscape exists, and its exploration is called
for. Anyone can obtain passage into its territories; no
one is forbidden entrance. But how deeply into this
strange realm you will travel and how many of its
sights and wonders you will see and experience is
solely dependent upon you. I can share only what I
have experienced thus far before I venture further.
Soon, perhaps, you will have your own experiences
to share.

2

Different Laws for a Different Realm

Every region and realm has its own laws and principles by which it operates. We cannot apply the rules by which we normally live our earthly lives to the environment in outer space; such a mistake could be catastrophic. The Dreamscape also operates in ways quite different from those by which we live in our daily, waking world. The laws and principles of gravity, mass, time, and space do not apply in the same way in the environment of dreams, and if we try to make them apply we will fail to understand what is occurring.

If you wish to be more than a stranger within the Dreamscape then you must study its laws, customs, rules, and principles of operation—just as you would if you were to take up residence in a foreign country on this planet. Of course it is not necessary that you know all the mechanics of the Dreamscape's laws anymore than it is necessary for you to be a physicist in order to get along in physical reality. But just as you cannot throw a baseball to the catcher without taking gravity and velocity into consideration, so you cannot comprehend what is going on in your dreams without some knowledge of the basic laws of the

Dreamscape. In this chapter I discuss those principles you must grasp before you can achieve a beginning understanding of the way things operate in your dreams. Later I will go into greater depth regarding the nature of the dream environment, since further exploration requires deeper understandings.

You alone will have to deal with the particulars of your own experience; I cannot explore for you, nor can anyone else. Until you pass beyond the realm wherein you create your private dreams we cannot exchange information about mutually shared experiences. Certain principles, however, will be common to all our ventures, and we all have basically the same equipment with which to work.

DREAM MEMORIES AND THEIR SYMBOLIC NATURE

When you first begin exploring the Dreamscape most if not all of your dealings will be with memories. Due to the nature of the earth-attuned mind and our identification with it, we do not know how to employ the focus of consciousness necessary to be self-aware within the Dreamscape. But this is not the only reason for us to work strictly with dream memories at first.

Generally, throughout our daily lives our conscious awareness is absorbed in what is happening each moment. For example, during a heated argument you are caught up with your emotions, especially your emotional reactions. In such a situation you are not cool and rational enough to think out what your wisest or most apt remarks would be. Later, when the event has passed, you can look back on it and assess it more clearly. You might be able to see why you were angered, what you should have said, and how you think you should have acted or reacted. So, dealing with events and experiences after the fact is really not foreign to us. In fact, more often than we might like to admit, we are no more self-aware in waking reality than we are in dreaming reality. It is just that our waking reality seems to have more continuity.

If you can forget yourself in an argument, while reading a book, or watching a movie, is it any wonder that you forget yourself during the often fantastic experiences in your dreams? As you attain greater understanding of the ways in which consciousness operates within the dream environment you will achieve greater self-awareness. With further evaluation you will begin to see that your life within the dream environment has its own continuity.

In working with memories of experiences in the Dreamscape, the first rule is: do not take what you remember of your travels literally. This should be obvious, but to many people it is not. Many of the images and events recalled from dreams are symbols which represent something other than what they appear to be on the surface. It may be maintained that the same is true of images we perceive in waking reality, but an acceptance of this aspect is not required for an understanding of the order within the Dreamscape.

One of the reasons these symbols should not be taken literally is that often what you experience within the dream environment is so foreign to physical reality that it cannot be understood from an earth-focused perspective. For this reason, if you are to recall anything at all of the experience, it must be translated into recognizable symbols which represent, but do not perfectly convey, the contents of your dream experience. It is as if you were to attempt to translate classical Latin into English. The essential meaning would translate, but the tone, rhythm, and imagery of the original language would be lost. Therefore, it is up to you to glean the essence of your experience from the symbols with which you are provided; to take them literally would be to allow the deeper meanings to elude you.

The language of symbols may be more appropriate in the dream experience because your dreaming consciousness interrelates with concepts, feelings, and energies more than it does with the particulars of the isolated objects and events. These gestalts of experience then are translated into physical terms which convey the experience in more manageable packages. Everything that we experience, whether in the dreaming or waking environment, must be filtered through our minds in order for us to deal with it in terms suitable to our present states of consciousness.

Remember, however, that not all dreams are of a specifically symbolic nature. Those which relate most closely to our daily lives will more nearly approximate our usual types of experiences. For example: If you are trying to decide whether you should accept a certain job offer, you might first dream that you do so; following this you might encounter a series of experiences that convey to you to some degree the likely outcome of such a choice. Then you might dream that you do not take the job, and following this would come dreams showing another set of circumstances. A good portion of such dreams might be experienced in a guise that does not need to be probed for deeper meaning. A small portion may or may not involve scenarios which need to be interpreted to reveal levels of resulting value, fulfillment, or disappointment that come from taking the job. You have to learn to discriminate between what needs to be evaluated symbolically and what should be taken simply for what it appears to be.

The Principle of Association

We use particular images to represent certain feelings or concepts according to the principle of association. Close your eyes and think of peace. What images come to your mind? A clear lake surrounded by shade-giving trees? A meadow of flowers? Your grand-mother rocking you by the fireplace when you were a child? Whatever image comes to your mind when you think of peace is the image that presently rep-resents this state to you. The image likely will change with time, so that you will use a different symbol to represent peace as your attitudes change, but the principle remains the same: you associate a particular image with a corresponding feeling or concept.

Within the Dreamscape this type of symbol-making and symbol-using goes on all the time. What you often perceive in your private dreams are symbols you have used to instantaneously manifest and rep-resent your inner feelings and conceptualizations. For instance, on occasion you might have a strong desire to experience the feelings associated with absolute freedom. In waking reality you cannot always do this, but in the dream environment you are free to expe-rience whatever you please. Perhaps you dream of riding a horse through open countryside, or you might dream of flying with the birds. It's up to you to choose the scenario that best gives rise to the feelings you seek to experience.

Play a little game with yourself. Consider a few objects or images one at a time, contemplate them, and see what kinds of feelings or ideas are evoked. For example, what feelings or thoughts do you get when you think of a horse, a bat, a fire, a fountain, or a meadow? You will find that corresponding associations arise with each of these images. If you do this long enough you will find that each image takes you into a series of associations. Your mind will create a chain of associations which your focus of attention can follow as you would follow the course of a dream. You might think of a horse in an open field, followed by a herd of horses, mountains in the background, an eagle soaring above it all, and the sun shining brightly in the sky, followed by an image of the night sky with its spaciousness and beauty. Such a string of associations can go on endlessly, but the associations are not always so easily recognizable. Images from your past may jump in, or thoughts of some person with whom you have not communicated in years.

Association knows no boundaries of time or place. Often associative images arise from unconscious regions so that we do not even recognize their connection with whatever else we have been thinking about or feeling. Association can take you all over the place in the twinkling of an eye.

So it is with dreams. Without the constrictions of time and space you can and do have dreams that jump around through a series of images and events which, when taken as a group, appear to be totally disordered and random. But when viewed in the light of their association with each other they become a quite understandable series of symbols and images. It takes effort, however, to unravel the paths by which any set of symbols are associated.

When we say that the images of our dream memories are disordered we are forgetting how our minds habitually work. We would like to think, perhaps, that our minds are rational, logical, and proceed in a direct line from one thought to another. But we have only to observe our mental machinations for a short while to see just how disordered and meandering, from a strictly logical viewpoint, our thoughts really are. Most of us have fairly undisciplined minds, and if we were given the task of consciously following the paths they travel in the course of an hour we would find it nearly impossible to accomplish. Thus, we cannot condemn the Dreamscape for seeming to be disordered when it is we who create what we perceive.

Furthermore, we are relative beginners in the art of understanding dreaming. If we were to travel to a foreign land we would be ignorant of the customs and rules of behavior in force there, and so we undoubtedly would make our share of social blunders. Likewise, we are unfamiliar with many of the rules and customs in the Dreamscape, and we cannot blame this realm because we seem to manage haphazardly.

Just as we do not behave from a fully conscious state during our daily lives, often settling into a routine and losing ourselves in it, or reacting to situations automatically rather than acting from a conscious overview, so do we rarely participate in the dream environment from a fully aware state. With practice you can learn to be more conscious while dreaming; then the wonders and possibilities of the Dreamscape become truly marvelous. But before you can do that you must learn more about how things work there.

The principle of association plays an important part, not only in any successful interpretation of dream experiences, but also in the creation of our private dreams. In the conscious or unconscious creation of any dream scenario your consciousness is quite creative and playful. It sees no value in limiting a creation to one format or form when a variety of interposed images and events will accomplish the purpose more completely and effectively. Your

dreaming focus of consciousness is better equipped
to handle a wide variety of stimuli simultaneously
than is your waking focus of consciousness, which is
narrowly focused on one band of experience necessarily. Therefore, a variety of symbols may be employed within one scenario which, when seen from
an earth-attuned perspective, are poorly related, but
from a dreaming-consciousness perspective are perfectly and clearly related.

A full series of dreams may be initiated through
association. You may create a scenario that represents
a current problem in your state of daily affairs, then
after it is completed find yourself dreaming about
other problems which are linked with the original
one. Or you may create a fantasy adventure purely
for the fun of it, which in turn might initiate further
fantasies that are freely played out. The tangents, side
issues, past issues, and related scenarios that may be
initiated through association are endless. Obviously,
if you wish to understand your dream scenarios you
must do the work of sorting through these associations. Just as you could not determine the ecological
balances of a strange land without studying the parts
played by each of its inhabitants, so you cannot
understand the balances of your dream scenarios
without understanding the component parts and their
functions.

THE MUTABILITY OF CONSCIOUSNESS

There is another aspect of dreaming consciousness
which cannot be ignored if we are to learn our way
around this fabulous Dreamscape. Consciousness, as
it manifests itself within the dream environment, is
highly mutable. Have you ever dreamed of yourself
as being of the opposite sex, or that you looked very

different from the way you do in waking, physical reality? You may have even dreamed that you were some sort of animal. Just as you can imagine yourself any way that you wish, so can you create yourself in any form within the dream environment. Within the Dreamscape reality is as free as the imagination.

This mutability of consciousness allows us even greater freedoms of creativity and experience, especially in the more subjective realms of the Dreamscape. We are free not only to imagine what it would be like to be a person of a different sex or another race, we actually can enact it. We are free to identify with anyone or anything much more completely this way. Since the consciousness in the dream environment is not dependent upon a particular form it is free to experience any form.

Your dreaming consciousness allows you to be an observer, participant, or both within any scenario. Just as you can watch a movie and still be fully aware of other events transpiring in your vicinity, so can the dreaming consciousness create a scenario and then remain somewhat detached from it in order to observe the situation dispassionately. And, as you can immerse yourself so fully in a movie that you don't know what the person next to you is saying, so can you, in the context of a dream, become so caught up in the events taking place before you that you lose the perspective of a detached observer. If you choose to experience a scenario more directly, you can shift "roles" and become one of the characters, subsequently losing the perspective of observer. Or you can do both. This flexibility is the natural condition of your dreaming consciousness, so you must be aware of it as you attempt dream interpretation; otherwise you will get lost trying to figure out where *you* were within the dream.

UNRAVELING THE COMPLEXITIES OF DREAMING

Another factor we occasionally encounter in the dreaming state is the simultaneity of time, that is, two or more dream scenarios occurring at the same time. This is not an easy concept to comprehend, locked as we usually are in a linear-time framework. But we must recognize that it is possible for us to have more than one dream at a time. At this stage, it does not matter whether you call it simultaneity of time or the ability of consciousness to divide itself. What matters is that you recognize the possibility that your memories of a dream may involve recalling overlapping dreams, thus leading to further confusion. Often, there will be an association between these overlapping dreams, but it is easier for the beginning explorer of the Dreamscape to deal with one dream scenario at a time. If you recognize the possibility of simultaneous dreams you will be better prepared for confusing memories from the dream environment.

Not all dreams are private. Many, in fact, are co-operative ventures, just as waking reality is a cooperative venture. Another person may appear unexpectedly on the scene, thus breaking the relative continuity of your dream. Or, you may be involved in a drama that involves the participation of various personalities, each choosing to work through this drama for his or her own reason. My experience leads me to believe that these people are not necessarily my own creations but sometimes really are other entities participating in the dream. Therefore, not all dream experiences can be interpreted solely in the light of our own symbol-meanings. Some of these situations will be discussed in more detail later when we get into the various aspects of dreaming.

Finally, it must be remembered that not all experiences in the Dreamscape take shape according to the intentions of one or more individuals. It is possible to experience levels of the Dreamscape where its objective reality plays the prominent role, where what we perceive is not as dramatically colored by our own creations. In this case what we see will appear in the same guise to everyone who visits there and will remain the same whether or not anyone is present. Since the scenarios involved are not purely self-created, any attempt to interpret your experiences in them in the light of total subjectivity would result in misunderstanding and error. You must know where you are in the Dreamscape in order to interpret what you experience.

All of these factors make it difficult to come to the heart of the nature of the Dreamscape, but we would be remiss if we failed to take them into account. An oversimplified approach to the interpretation of dreaming experiences would leave us with a shallow understanding, not only of isolated dreams, but also of the complexities and depths of consciousness. However, the task is not insurmountable. We do have reliable tools with which to work.

Using Your Intuition

In interpreting our experiences in the dream environment we must learn to employ our faculties of intuition. If we try to deduce dreams from a logical standpoint we are attempting to apply physical reality rules to nonphysical reality. Intuition is a subtler and more ephemeral faculty, and is perfectly suited to the investigation of dreams and the dream environment. It allows subtle associations to rise to the surface of consciousness unimpeded by the logical intellect which has a tendency to explain away anything that does not fit into its established framework. The intellect is an essential and powerful tool, but it is not capable of exploring all aspects of reality. Once the intuition has been allowed to present its findings, then the intellect can go about categorizing and organizing those findings in relationship to physical reality.

Often we have no idea where the information our intuition presents to us comes from and cannot explain rationally how we received the information. We must not be so prejudiced as to reject ideas simply because they have not been arrived at in a logical manner. The inner senses reach into areas where the logical mind cannot go, and the intuition, as we know it, is our rudimentary contact with those inner senses.

We have trained ourselves to ignore much of the information that is available to us. In order to make use of this lost information we first must believe that it exists and that we can access it. Then we have to watch and listen for it, subsequently recognizing and using it when it does arrive. In this way we are encouraging our intuition to become more active in our lives.

Interpreting Symbols

Symbols are often very personal. From any single symbol or image different people may derive or discover different associations. A deep lake might mean peace and profundity to one person, yet convey helplessness and terror to another; and it may mean all of these things to someone else. All that we have experienced in our lives plays a significant part in determining what kinds of associations we make to any symbol. Of course, there are archetypal symbols which represent generally the same concepts to everyone, but it is best to deal with the private, more personal symbols first.

Anything in a dream can be taken as a symbol because everything can be associated with, and is associated with, many other things. An image may represent one thing when applied to daily life, but quite another when applied to the mysteries of the evolution of personal consciousness. It may involve yet other associations when related to your personal purpose in life. Such levels can be pursued indefinitely.

Not all symbols and encountered images, however, require interpretation on all levels—or on any level at all—though increased insight can always be gained by looking into deeper meanings for everything that we experience. It is not necessary, however, or even advisable, to explore the hidden significances of every tree you see, for example. Nor is it necessary, in examining the memory of a dream, to investigate every possible association it might evoke. It depends on what you perceive as the *primary significance* of the dream, and what you are striving to get out of it. You could spend your entire life probing the mysteries of a single dream, or a single life event for that matter, since everything ultimately is connected to everything else. You will have greater success if you stick to exploring the primary lessons and insights that any particular dream scenario is relating. You recall these dreams because there is some particularly relevant insight involved which applies to your present state of consciousness and to the present dilemmas with which you are faced.

In the course of this book I will go into greater depth regarding the "laws" of the dream environment. I also will probe the mysteries of symbols further. But at this point you need some personal material with which to work, so that you can begin developing techniques for increasing your participation in the activities that take place in the Dreamscape. Personal experience will do far more to enhance your understanding than talk will.

3

Getting Acquainted with
Your Dreaming Self

Everyone, to one degree or another, has a variety of experiences within the Dreamscape. What we recall of these experiences is usually not an exact representation of what actually took place, but for our present purposes of exploration and interpretation these partial memories will suffice. Most people neither remember nor investigate most of their dreams. The serious explorer of the dream environment, however, must not only study these experiences, he or she also must strive to recall as many of them as possible. Eventually you will find yourself investigating aspects of the dream environment and experiences within it other than your recollections of private dreams. But establishing a familiarity with the ways in which your consciousness interrelates with the Dreamscape and with the meanings of your private dreams is a necessary prerequisite to any understanding of the more alien dimensions and the phenomena encountered at deeper levels.

RECORDING YOUR DREAMING EXPERIENCES

When exploring any new region one must attempt to keep an accurate record of the sights, impressions, and inhabitants encountered along the way. In a realm where nearly everything is unfamiliar this is especially important. Some researchers maintain that recording dreams is a mistake because it leads us to separating ourselves from the experience by objectifying it. To some degree this is true, but it is better to record something and thereby have access to it than to forget it altogether.

Each of us has experienced the phenomenon of recalling a dream upon awakening, but forgetting it after a few short moments. This happens especially if we have to arise immediately and prepare for the day's activities. Unless we record what we remember as soon as possible we invariably will lose touch with it. Occasionally, of course, we have dreams of such a striking nature that we just can't forget them, but for the most part we have systematically trained ourselves to let our dream memories slip away.

Ideally one would awaken after each significant dream and record every detail of it immediately, but this is impractical. The next best thing is to record your dreams, or what you remember of them, upon first awakening in the morning. In practice, however, this too can be difficult because as you progress in your dreamwork you will begin to remember more and more dreams, and recording each detail of each dream is a time-consuming process. A technique I have found useful is to write down the key elements of each dream upon awakening. Then, when time permits, I detail the dreams more completely in my journal. The notes you jot down initially will bring the dream back to you, though perhaps not always in full detail, and you can fill in features and information you did not have time to record at first. At the same time any insights into your dreams' deeper meanings can be recorded.

If you are so inclined you might experiment with using a tape recorder. Some people find it easier to record their dreams this way than to awaken fully and write them down legibly and coherently. Whether you write your dreams or record them on tape, you may discover that as your explorations progress, and as you begin to experience more and more things you wish to remember, you will find the necessary motivation to awaken from time to time during the night in order to record your dreams more completely and accurately.

Location

When recording your dreams there are quite a number of things to note. I suggest beginning with your surroundings, the appearance of the location where your experience takes place. Is it a place you recognize, or is it a totally unfamiliar location? Is the dream set in a house, a restaurant, an office building, or is the site undecipherable? Try to picture the dream in your mind and recall elements in the dream scene. You may find that the location is similar to a place with which you are familiar, yet in the dream it appears somewhat different. Make note of both the similarities and the differences. Often a dream takes place in a vehicle, such as an automobile or an airplane; in this case, the vehicle qualifies as the location. Give as detailed a description of the scenery as possible. Remember that in the recollection of any dreaming experience what you might think of at first as an insignificant detail could yield pertinent meaning for you later.

The locations where your dreaming experiences occur are not just ephemeral visions which disappear when you cease to dream about them. In many cases you encounter places to which you return again and again. These places are, of course, not physical, but they nevertheless exist. Because these regions are not physical but composed of the energy of the Dreamscape, they can change in appearance and still be recognizable. These places do not have a spatial relationship to one another as physical places do, as I stated earlier; somehow more than one location can exist in the same "place." Therefore, recording the location of your dream experiences not only affords material for personal interpretation; eventually it can also yield a kind of map.

Other People

Make note of anyone you encounter in your dreams. Are they familiar faces or do they appear to be strangers? Do they seem to be people you know, but do not recognize? Are they individuals you know, yet they look different somehow? How clear were their faces to you? The relative clarity of the other individuals' characteristics could give you valuable clues as to how important they are in your dream. Not all beings have a personality focused in physical reality. In the Dreamscape interaction can take place between all manner of individuals. Many people you encounter in dreams represent different aspects of your own consciousness. You may also encounter the dream forms of people you know in physical reality and even some that you know only in the dream environment. (I discuss dream forms in Chapter 4.) Beings originating from other realities altogether may interact with you. So you have to keep a record of your interactions if you wish to understand who you are dealing with in any dream scenario.

Many times your dreams will contain no one else,

only yourself and scenery, or animals. There may even be times when you experience scenarios where nothing is distinct visually. But in these cases did you hear or smell something? Was some strong feeling or impression dominant in the experience? All of these things should be recorded.

The senses used within the Dreamscape are necessarily different from those used in physical reality, but for each of the physical senses there is a corresponding inner sense. Also, the feelings, moods, and tones you encounter may seem strange. This is natural. Once again, recording everything helps you to acquaint yourself with the differences.

Your Role

Consider also your role in the dream. Were you a participant or an observer? Did your roles change in the course of the dream? Do you know what you looked like? Were you an adult or a child? Were you involved in the action of the dream, or were you just tagging along with someone else?

In the dream environment you can be whomever you choose. You can assume whatever roles suit your interests. You can exit the scene while the character with whom you first identified continues the action as a separate entity. Be alert to your changes of perspective. Anything else you can think of in relation to the part you played or the identity you maintained within the dream should be recorded.

Events

Next, try to record a detailed description of the events which took place. At times you will find it hard to determine the order in which things happened. Scattered images may occur to you without any recognizable sequence. Many times, however, the dream will have an obvious sequence of events. Leave nothing out in your descriptions. You will find that as you concentrate on the dream you will remember even more of it than you did upon first awakening. Where did you go? What did you do? What did you say? What did others say to you? Was someone with you all the time, or part of the time? What did you see, hear, smell, feel, or taste? Did you think about anything? Did something transform into something else?

Time is much different in the Dreamscape, and when we are forced to recall the images in a linear-time sequence we encounter many confusing elements. If you have had several dreams simultaneously, how are you to recall and make sense of them except by translating the experience into a sequential order the intellect can understand? When you do this, however, you are often left with jumbled memories. Don't demand that your recollections of your dreaming experiences come to you in what you term a logical, sequential order. Just record the information as you recall it; even in its apparently mixed-up order it can reveal much on examination.

Time can manifest in a variety of ways within the Dreamscape. More will be said about this later. For now it is important to remember that you should not force your dream recollections to comply with the way events transpire in waking reality. If you force an unnatural order on your dreaming experiences you may eliminate any possibility of seeing into their true meanings.

Remember that anything is possible in the dream environment. Don't dismiss something just because it seems bizarre or impossible in terms of your waking experience. The criterion of what is and what isn't possible within the dream environment is far different from that of your personal waking life.

Your encounters while dreaming can be disorienting, especially when viewed in the context of physical reality. A chair can turn into a horse as easily as a caterpillar changes into a butterfly. Water can burn and mountains can sink into the earth. You can fly or swim through the depths of the earth. Someone can die and then get up and walk away. You can experience existence as a dog or as the wind. Be prepared for anything, and make no value judgments based on the way events accord with your usual concept of reality. The important thing at first is simply to record everything you can remember about your dreams.

If you recall a series of dreams try to note in what order they occurred. If you cannot do this at least note in what order you recalled them. Often the line that separates one dream from another is indiscernible; the transition from one scenario to another can be so smooth that you will think of them as one dream. Other times the transition is startlingly dramatic. Remember that in your waking life events are not distinctly separated from each other either. The things that you experience in life run into one another; you experience a stream of events. In the same manner dreams can run into each other so that you are simply left with a string of images. In time you will begin to recognize the chains of association as well as the breaks in relative continuity. We all have to begin somewhere and recording everything you remember, as clearly as possible, is a good start.

Beginning to Interpret Your Dreams

As you are recording each dream notice any feelings, impressions, reactions, or thoughts which surface in relation to it. A dream with the simplest of elements may elicit strong emotions as you record it. Thoughts may occur to you which at the time seem to have nothing to do with the dream itself. It does no harm to record everything that occurs to you while you are investigating a dream; later you may be able to separate the pertinent material from that which does not apply to the dream. Sometimes you immediately get a feeling for what the dream was all about, or for some of the hidden meanings within it. Be sure to make note of these. If you have time while you are recording your dreams try to follow any feelings or intuitive insights which may occur to you; such things can lead you down the path of greater understanding.

Often, the best time to delve into the meaning of a dream is when it is freshest in your memory. At that time your consciousness is still fairly close to the experience and is better able to strike upon the dream's ramifications. Of course, you won't always have the time to follow everything to where it's leading you, but when you do have the luxury of time you'll find doing so is very beneficial in your exploration of the Dreamscape. Once a dream is well recorded you have laid conscious claim to the experiences contained therein. Dreams can reveal insights and meanings even years later.

Once you have recorded a dream experience and wish to attempt some interpretation, use your notes to refresh your memory of the experience before you begin. Then if any immediate and obvious meanings come to you write them down. If nothing comes take a few moments just to "hang out" with the dream, to relive it. Be alert to any subtle, or not so subtle, feeling tones which arise. What was the overall mood? Was the lighting bright or dark; was the general tone of the dream light or dark? Did you enjoy having the dream, or was it an unpleasant experience?

See if you can detect any principal theme in the dream scenario. Was there a connecting thread of danger, of wish-fulfillment, or perhaps of inspiration? Did the experience seem to be dealing with an intellectual, emotional, spiritual, or physical theme? Examine these things lightly and playfully. Don't approach this exercise with a penetrating logic; if you do you will make your mind too rigid in its approach and you will likely close it off to subtleties. Don't think of your attempts at interpretation as critical; this is not a test which you can either pass or fail. Approach it as a joyful experiment in the exploration of your own creations and experiences. From the point of view of your dreaming consciousness, existence and experience are not life and death matters. They are the essence of joy and creativity conjoined with self-discovery.

After you've spent a little time hanging out with the whole experience of your dream and have noted any impressions that occurred to you, begin to look at the various elements of the dream. Examine the individual images and events that you found and recalled. You'll find that some aspects don't seem important at all, while others will be so odd or so striking that you'll know they must be telling you something. For the time being you might work only with those elements which seem most important or striking to you; you'll probably have the most success in eliciting further insights from these. Later, perhaps, some of the less significant or less obvious factors will reveal themselves as playing more important roles.

Take any symbol or image and let it float about in your mind. (It is of little use to give examples here since the possibilities are endless.) What associations come to you? What thoughts or feelings do you find arising in conjunction with this image? Write them all down.

If you don't find any personal associations with the image you're investigating, can you think of any associations which traditionally have been connected with it? A house might represent your psyche with the rooms symbolizing its various sections or regions and the floor levels corresponding to the unconscious, conscious, and superconscious. Bear in mind the traditional correspondences with the four elements: water with emotion, fire with spirit or vitality, earth with matter or body, air with thoughts. Many animals have traditional associations as well: fox with cunning, horse with spirit, eagle with spirit, bat with powers of darkness, snake with serpent power or kundalini. Even though these may not be associations you would normally make, it can be helpful to bear in mind the influences of myths and symbols that have come to have fairly common meanings and associations in our culture.

Remember that in the Dreamscape associations play the most important role, not the sequence of events. You are dealing with a realm that is unrestricted by time or place. You can travel instantaneously from here to there or from now to then. Follow the associations and you will be moving through the dream environment.

Gradually, then, go to the next images in the dream and do the same sort of thing. You may find that there is a common thread of association with a number of these images; this could be a key to the basic elements running through the dream experience. Always be alert to those associations which feel most applicable at the time.

Not all associations will apply to any given symbol all the time. It is up to you to use your intuition to strike upon those which do relate to the dream you are interpreting. In time you will learn to recognize your own feelings of rightness about any associations or interpretations you make in regard to a dream or an image.

Bear in mind that there will always be dreams which seem closed to interpretation. Sometimes they will be so simple that you will be tempted to dismiss them as a nothing but the playing out of a fantasy. At other times they seem so bizarre and so foreign or complicated that you don't know where to begin. Don't worry about this. If a dream is too hard a nut to crack just let it alone. It is not necessary that you find deep meanings in every experience. Remember that you're gathering information, and that in time when you have more information a wider view will allow you to put smaller elements into perspective. Or in time something may happen in your waking life which will provide a key to understanding a dream that was before uninterpretable. Precognitive dreams especially are hard to recognize until what they preview unfolds. Later, when you understand your dreams better, you may begin to recognize elements within dreams which alert you to their possible precognitive nature.

From time to time reread your dream journal and write down any new ideas or interpretations or feelings that come to you. At this time you can record any correspondences between your dreams and your daily life which have become clear. You may find that something as simple as a book you are reading or a movie you watch one night somehow relates to a dream and has special meaning for you. Reexamining your dream journal will help you get a feel for the pattern of dream activities which take place. Quite likely you will begin to catch correspondences between separate dreams, too. In my dream journal I have recorded and interpreted years of experience.

Rereading it frequently has proven to be one of the most valuable methods for coming to an understanding of the activities in which I am engaged in the Dreamscape.

As your journal grows begin to make note of those elements which recur in your dreams. Are there certain people who appear often? Are there places to which you go again and again? Is there a period in which you had only happy dreams, or only sad ones? If you notice periods where the dreams are similar, try to remember what was going on in your life at that time and see if it corresponds to these dreams in some way. Also, are certain symbols frequently encountered? Do you often dream of animals, or fires, or storms? If you notice recurring symbols record them on a separate sheet and investigate their associations further. Remember that you will seldom discover things if you don't do any explorations. The more time you spend prospecting for gold the more likely you are to find it.

I also suggest that you keep a second journal and record in it what is going on in your day-to-day waking life. So many of our dreams relate to what we are experiencing in physical reality that a comparison between these two sets of experiences is invaluable. You may not recognize inner crises when they are occurring, but later they may become evident. Then you can go back and look at both of your journals and see how you were dealing with that crisis in both realms. Numerous other insights also can be gained through this technique.

As you progress in your studies and interpretations you will begin to see what methods and approaches work best for you. Be prepared and willing to make whatever changes are necessary in your methods. If you have been trying to interpret dreams immediately on awakening but find that you get better results if you wait until later, then by all means let the dreams wait a while before you examine them. No one wants to waste time in unfruitful pursuits. And applying yourself to a method that yields little or no results will only discourage you. The same holds true with the way you record your dreams or enter them in your journal. Let intuition and experience guide you into the best methods for you. You are a pioneer and it is up to you to find the best trail through the new territory.

INFLUENCING YOUR DREAMS

In addition to recording and interpreting your dreams there are other things you can do to increase your conscious participation in and understanding of your dream experiences. Since dreams often relate to or are triggered by events from waking reality, it should be easy to recognize that you can have some influence over what you dream by applying effort while you are awake. One of the most effective approaches to influencing your nightly experiences and creations is simple suggestion. A suggestion is a command you give to yourself in order to bring about a desired result. Suggestions can have a strong bearing on your relationship to the Dreamscape, especially if given just prior to going to sleep.

If you do not feel that you are remembering enough dreams try gently suggesting to yourself before you fall asleep either that you will awaken after significant dreams so that you can record them, or that on awakening in the morning you will recall your dreams. Do this regularly for best results. Since previously you may not have devoted much time and energy to recalling your experiences in the dream environment, it is only natural that you now might have to put a little effort into changing your habits. It can also be helpful at this time to gently remind yourself that you have good reason for recalling dreams; they contain valuable experiences, they afford new insights, they increase your understanding of the depths of reality, and you desire to explore this realm. In addition to the presleep suggestion that you will recall your dreams you can tell yourself on awakening that you want to remember more of your dreams. This reinforces the presleep suggestion. It may take a little time for these suggestions to work, but be patient—they will.

Often events of the day will stimulate the recollection of a particular dream. When this happens be sure to record not only the dream, but if possible, the event or situation which keyed its remembrance.

You also can make more specific suggestions regarding the actual content of your dreams. If there is a particular problem with which you are dealing suggest before sleep that you have a dream or a series of dreams in which you explore the problem and gain insights into its possible solutions. You may not always remember whether or not you had success in this, but even though you may not remember the particular dream in which you dealt with the problem, trust that you did so. Be open during the course of the following days for any new insights to your problem that may surface in your conscious mind or in your feelings. Solutions can manifest as a result of dreamwork even if you do not recall the dream itself.

You can encourage insights and increased understanding about yourself and your waking reality by suggesting pertinent dreams. If you have a decision to make you can explore possible courses of action in your dreams. If you have a health problem you can suggest a dream that examines the problem and its remedy. Healing can take place through therapeutic dreams. The possibilities are endless, and there is no reason why we should not take advantage of them.

You may find that you need to work on the proper wording or tone of your suggestions in order to increase your level of success. You may be trying to command your psyche too forcefully, bullying it, so to speak. On the other hand your suggestions may be too weak and lack conviction. Experiment with these things and then make changes to suit your own temperament and needs.

Finally, when you feel up to it, begin regularly suggesting to yourself that you will be more conscious within the dream environment, that you will bring more of your consciousness to bear upon the experiences you have in the Dreamscape. You may want to suggest that you actually "come awake" within a dream, arriving at a state of consciousness in which you know you are dreaming. (This is known as "lucid" dreaming and it will be explored in more depth in a later chapter.) In any case, an increased focus of consciousness within the dream environment will increase your dreaming effectiveness and also will enhance your abilities to recall what you dream.

In addition to these suggestions it is helpful on occasion to take the time to examine your beliefs regarding dreams. Be honest with yourself in facing any fears you might have about uncovering hidden aspects of your nature. Ask yourself what you believe about your dreams and the dream environment; then examine the basis for those beliefs. If you have negative attitudes regarding dreams and dream recall you will have to work these out or they will impede your efforts. If you have any fears about exploring the unknown, these too will have to be resolved. Or if you simply lack any positive beliefs about the dream environment you may have to institute them: tell yourself that you believe you will be rewarded through pursuing an exploration of the Dreamscape.

One more method for increasing your understanding of the dream reality should be considered. On occasion you may have experienced what might be called a half-waking, half-sleeping state. Often when we lie in bed prior to sleep we drift into a semisleep state in which we retain some of our normal waking consciousness but are softly experiencing the beginnings of dreams. These fleeting images have been termed *hypnagogic images* by psychologists and dream researchers. In this state of consciousness you can successfully observe the formation of dreams while you are still partially awake.

In truth, there are several stages of "going to sleep." In each of these you move deeper into the dreaming environment. Generally you slide into sleep without noticing these phases, but with effort and intent it is fairly easy to recognize and observe at least the first phase. You will notice that at a certain point your conscious attention seems to turn inward and you begin to forget about your body. You may feel as if you are floating within your mind. Often you will find yourself running through the experiences of the day. Images will begin to form in your mind with increasing vividness. At this point it is common to slide right into sleep, but with a little effort you will find that you can hold your consciousness at this level and actually watch yourself forming and encountering dream images.

This half-sleeping, half-waking state of consciousness is a platform from which many uncommon experiences can be initiated, and they are discussed farther on. For now, just try to be aware of changes in your consciousness as you begin to go to sleep. Try to observe the inner workings of your psyche. This also is a perfect time to make any determined suggestions regarding your dreams, since at this stage you are already halfway there.

In time you will gain a considerable body of material from your explorations of the Dreamscape. Quantity, of course, is not necessarily better than quality. But for the initial purposes of exploring the dream environment the more experiences of which you are aware, the better your chances of understanding the material are. A few snapshots of a foreign land won't acquaint you with its character the way several trips to the region would. With enough material on your own dreaming activities you will begin to get a good feel for how things work in the Dreamscape. Through continued efforts at interpretation, you'll also learn more about how you relate to different symbols and images. And you'll grow more proficient at recognizing diverse aspects of dreaming experience and various types of dreams, thus enabling you to interpret them more accurately.

As we cover the various aspects of dreaming experience we'll go more into what to look for. Different types of dreams have different feelings associated with them, as well as different sets of imagery. But you can't interpret your dream experiences unless you recall them and record them. This is your first task.

There will be days, weeks, even months when you won't remember many dreams. And there will be periods in which you just don't have the motivation to record dreams or to interpret them. This is natural. There are rhythms and cycles in our consciousness, and there are times when it is not proper for us to explore the Dreamscape. At these times you may be called on to concentrate all your energies on what is going on in your physical reality. But the time will come when your dream recall increases and when your motivation for further forays into the Dreamscape is on the rise. Follow your own cycles and don't try to force the issue. And don't be discouraged by the ups and downs of your search and exploration; these are as natural as the ups and downs of daily waking life.

The Multidimensional Nature of Consciousness

Perhaps you are wondering how your consciousness can operate simultaneously in the physical realm and in the Dreamscape, especially during those times when the waking consciousness is not aware of the "dreamer's" activities. It may seem to you that at times you are awake, then as you go to sleep your consciousness changes and enters into another realm where things operate differently. From one perspective this is true. But from a greater perspective it is truer to say, as mentioned before, that you have many levels and aspects of consciousness operating simultaneously in various dimensions, and each is in communication with all of the others by one route or another.

We are multidimensional beings, but usually we identify with only one aspect of our consciousness, the aspect focused in physical reality. When we turn the attention in other directions we catch glimpses of other parts of our consciousness at work. One of the main reasons for exploring dreams and the Dreamscape is to become conscious of another dimension of ourselves, so that we can participate consciously in other aspects of our multidimensionality.

It is because we have more than one level to our consciousness that we can have dreams without recalling them. This is also why we can have a dream consciousness that knows quite adequately how to operate within the Dreamscape though our waking consciousness seems lost in that environment. We have trained ourselves to separate these aspects, but I believe the time is at hand when we must begin to reclaim the other aspects of our consciousness, to integrate these aspects into one whole, cohesive self. We focused our consciousness into the narrow band of waking reality in order to master that reality without the distractions inherent in other dimensions. But we are limited in how far we can go in mastering that reality so long as we consciously divorce ourselves from deeper portions of our own natures, and so long as we ignore the experiences we have in other objective realities.

Therefore, it is not so much that you alter your consciousness when you enter the Dreamscape; it is more accurate to say that while dreaming you attune yourself to the dreaming aspect of your consciousness. Each aspect is uniquely suited to navigate within its own system of reality, but these different aspects are more closely connected than most of us commonly think. By bringing more of the adventures of the dreaming consciousness through to the awareness of the waking consciousness we gradually remove the artificial boundary between them. When this is done each aspect of consciousness is better able to make use of the experiences of the other. The interpretation of dreams involves the waking consciousness coming to grips with the experiences of the dreaming consciousness, and thereby making more conscious use of those experiences.

An understanding of the symbology used and encountered within the Dreamscape enables us to attain greater knowledge of the symbology of our waking reality. It also enables the dreaming consciousness to serve the needs of the waking consciousness more effectively. And it allows us to communicate our physical-life purposes and needs to a portion of our consciousness which can help us reach our goals.

Part 2

4

On the Shores of the Dreamscape

The study and interpretation of dream experiences brings us face to face with much confusing information. It would be convenient if each dream came in a neatly bundled package, a simple unit which lent itself easily to a set of investigative methods. But the fact of the matter is that the material we gather through dreams is too alien to our accustomed way of relating to reality to permit this. Instead, it becomes necessary to examine the component parts of a dream, to isolate the individual elements and aspects and study these parts. Hopefully when we put them back together again they will form an understandable and cohesive unit which reveals the hidden meanings of the dream. Eventually it becomes more possible to look at a dream as a unit and immediately recognize its import, but in the beginning the divide–and–conquer approach seems best.

THE INTERWOVEN ASPECTS OF DREAMS

Dreams, like our experiences in waking reality, are not simple, one-line events. Each event or experience is interwoven with reality and touches our being in multiple ways. Even the activities we pursue solely for the purpose of entertainment in waking reality partake of different aspects: social, fantasy, adventure, mental, physical, and emotional. If we look we will find that there are always multiple aspects to any event or experience which affects our growth and learning. Dreams also partake of various aspects and carry import for us from a number of different angles.

Perhaps it would be fun to believe that every remembered dream experience is a highly symbolic key which when understood and used would unlock doors into the secrets of our inner selves or the universe. But this is not the case. There are dreams of this nature, of course, but there are also dreams which simply involve our consciousness in play, worry, fear, or any of the other not so sublime aspects of our natures. All of our experiences have value, and all of them reveal their value in unique ways.

Just as in waking reality we must learn to differentiate between various aspects of experience, so in dreaming experience we must do the same if we are to arrive at a clear understanding. In the physical environment we must know how to tell the difference, for example, between a scary movie and a truly dangerous life-situation. Otherwise we would be unable to deal with the illusion of danger the movie presents us, or we would fail to take appropriate action when actual danger threatens. We likewise have to know when we are fantasizing and when we are facing physical reality. To live as if fantasy were physical reality leads to mental aberrations.

In the Dreamscape we sometimes play and sometimes learn. Sometimes we observe the creations of others, sometimes we create our own situations, and sometimes we encounter realms which exist in their own right. Sometimes we fantasize purposefully for the delight and exploration of it, and sometimes we fantasize without knowing we are doing so. Sometimes we relate with imaginary beings, and sometimes we relate with beings who have their own independent existences.

While we are in the Dreamscape our dreaming consciousness is reasonably capable of making the necessary differentiations. It is when we bring the memory of our experiences through to our waking reality that we run into difficulty. Our waking perspective is not suited to differentiating between these aspects, and therefore we frequently form false interpretations. In attempting to interpret dreams our waking consciousness is trying to understand what our dreaming consciousness already knows.

It is because of our inability to recognize different aspects of dreaming experience that we find ourselves unable to distinguish, for example, between a precognitive dream of someone's physical death and a dream representing someone's inner transformations—or our own. By the same token we don't know if a dream about an automobile accident is a warning, the dream manifestation of a fear, or simply an adventure scenario. Does the experience of seeing a dog turn into a cat involve a lesson about mental faculties transferring their awareness to the emotional faculties, or is a wandering, playful consciousness simply juggling the elasticity of dream forms? The opportunities for such confusion grow even more numerous when we begin to deal, within the dream environment, with psychological problems, life decisions, past–life experiences, and symbolic consciousness interplays.

When we consider that in any one dream or dreaming scenario highly symbolic elements may be mixed with elements that are no more than what they appear to be, we can see how the potential for confusion is increased. Also, the consciousness can jump, without apparent transition, from the enactment of a psychological trauma to a fantasy role-playing adventure. These are but some of the reasons we cannot view a dream as a unit and categorize it as pure fantasy, pure adventure, or pure past-life experience. Not only are our recollections of these scenarios often sketchy or even inaccurate, but the experiences can blend in such a way as to partake of more than one aspect.

Consider the way the mind works. In many instances if someone were to ask you what you are thinking about, you would be able to answer with a half-dozen different things. Follow the course of your thoughts for the short space of a minute and see if they do not travel through a wide and varied territory. Unless you are concentrating deeply on one thing your mind rambles all over the place. Consider also that the consciousness—which I believe exists independent of the restrictions of time and place and is not limited to the experiences of one lifetime scenario—is even more free to wander and jump about through myriad channels and paths. In this light it is easy to see that we should never trap ourselves into simply attempting to interpret our dreams; what we are dealing with here is the nature of our dreaming consciousness as it relates to an environment that is foreign to our waking consciousness.

To be explorers of the Dreamscape we have to maintain a broad overview. We cannot become bogged down in any one dream experience, or in any sequence of dream experiences. We do need to investigate these, but at the same time we must examine the general nature of our consciousness as it is involved in these dreams. We cannot understand waking reality simply by looking at and categorizing all the things we see and experience in our lives; if we are to come to a clear understanding of our earthly experiences we must study ourselves and our relationships to what we experience. The same holds true when exploring and investigating the Dreamscape. Our primary goal is to become familiar with our dreaming consciousness, and we are attempting to do this by first interpreting and studying the experiences which the dreaming aspect of consciousness naturally encounters.

FANTASY AND ADVENTURE DREAMS

The interpretation of dreams is not as difficult as the above may suggest. It is necessary, however, that we guard against simplistic approaches to interpretation. With all of this in mind let's investigate some of those aspects of dreaming which are encountered early in the recollection of dreams.

Due to the inherent freedom manifested by consciousness within the Dreamscape we are able, in that environment, to play out any fantasy we might have. Within the dream environment time does not have the same finite, linear quality we perceive in our waking lives, so we literally have all the time in the world, and more, during which to express ourselves according to our infinite potentials and wide-ranging inclinations. It is only natural that we at times would employ the freedom of the dream environment for the purposes of unfolding our fantasies. All of us have desires which cannot be fulfilled in waking reality.

Fantasies take on many forms and these forms necessarily vary from individual to individual, but there are aspects to fantasy which we generally share. By nature we humans are an adventurous lot, though at times we may not think of ourselves in this way. All of us to one degree or another take pleasure in engaging in activities which challenge us and put us in touch with the deep vitality of existence. However, the life purposes and responsibilities we have chosen for ourselves often keep us from meeting with adventure on the scale that we might want or need for our peak fulfillment.

Fantasy dreams, as well as many other types of dreams, often have an aspect of adventure. Many times in the Dreamscape we encounter situations involving danger which we must either escape or face. All adventures, and all dreams containing adventure, bear some mark of danger, and this is one of the key features by which we can recognize the creation of adventure for the purposes of challenge within our dreams.

THE DREAM BODY

Within the Dreamscape, of course, we cannot be killed or even physically injured, since we are journeying in our dream bodies, not our physical ones. References to the concept of this dream body, the non-physical counterpart to the physical body, are encountered under varying terms in different cultures and ages. The ancient Egyptians believed in the *Ka* as well as other nonphysical parts of us that transcend death. In India we encounter the concept of the *Linga Sharira* and other subtle bodies which engage and contain the seven chakras. Western occultists acknowledge the "etheric body" and "astral body," made of subtle, superphysical matter. Europeans used to refer to the *doppelgänger* or the "body double." The Rosicrucians call it the "vital body," and the French spiritualists named it the *périsprit*.

Whether we call it the dream body, the astral body, or the spirit body of the shamans, we are talking about the vehicle of navigation used by consciousness to journey in nonphysical realms. At some stage in the evolution of consciousness we may find that we need no form at all around which to focus consciousness. But as we are now, whether for the purposes of securing a stable sense of self or for containing the "organs" of perception, we inevitably find ourselves "contained" within some form, some body. In the physical realm our physical bodies enable us to interact with the physical environment. In the Dreamscape we have nonphysical bodies which allow us to interact with that realm.

The dream body, then, is subject to the laws and conditions of the dream environment. It is affected by nonphysical stimuli and interacts with nonphysical objects and beings. It is not subject to physical conditions, however, such as physical injuries.

If our dream bodies are not liable to physical injuries, why do we dream of physical dangers? Why do we dream that someone is threatening us with bodily harm, for example, or that we are in peril as we climb a steep cliff? Aside from the often deeper symbolic connotations, our engagements with danger in the Dreamscape are often fantasy-adventure creations, and the images associated with physical danger serve the purpose of creating the atmosphere and psychological condition we need to elicit a sense of adventure to which we can relate easily.

Not all adventures in the Dreamscape, of course, are self-created. Inevitably you will experience or encounter objectively valid aspects of the Dreamscape, and such experiences necessarily will involve you with adventure and perhaps even with danger. But for now I want to discuss only those aspects of adventure in dreaming which you create for your own purposes.

When dreams contain elements of danger and adventure, of challenge and vitality, we seldom have trouble recognizing their nature, or at least that portion of their nature. On examining your dreams you should have little difficulty when it comes to recognizing situations or scenarios in which you are facing some challenge. Any dream in which there is a battle or an attempt to master some seemingly physical challenge partakes of the aspect of adventure to some degree. Of course, the images encountered within any adventure may have deeper meanings: a dream about climbing a mountain might represent the efforts required by ascending consciousness. But for now I want to stay with the simple aspect of adventure itself.

Why, then, do we seek adventure? Why do we manifest it in our dreams? First, overcoming challenges gives us a greater sense of our personal power. It increases our confidence and strengthens us. It puts us in touch with the vitality of existence, something we cannot always manage to do in waking reality. Finally, and perhaps most importantly, adventure and challenge are pathways to overcoming inner obstacles. When we climb a mountain we do not conquer the mountain, we conquer something within ourselves. In the Dreamscape when we defeat an opponent we actually may be overcoming some aspect of ourselves which was inhibiting our development.

We often use dream adventures to dramatize our encounters with self-limitations and to overcome them. Fears can be symbolized by anything from monsters to indistinct presences. By giving symbolic form to our self-limitations we enable ourselves to relate to and deal with what otherwise might be too intangible for us to grasp. Therefore, anytime you recognize some aspect of challenge and adventure in your dreams look to see if the obstacle or challenge which you faced represents something about yourself.

I am diverging a bit from the strictly adventure-some aspect of dreams. But as I said before all aspects are interconnected and we cannot adequately examine one without at least touching on others. However, in order to isolate the adventure aspects of a dream watch for challenge and danger. When you recognize these, attempt to determine whether the adventure simply involved the stimulation of what we might call "dream adrenaline" and the increase of a sense of personal power, or whether in addition to these things it contained symbolic images which represented something about you. For example, using the mountain-climbing image again, you simply may be engaging in fantasy and adventure, or you also may be exploring the ever-continuing ascent of your own nature, which can be seen as an ascent through the vast and ever-rising realms of reality.

If you find yourself engaging in the same adventure repeatedly, or if you face the same symbolic obstacle over and over again, then you must look deeper than the surface implications of adventure. Any recurring dream is trying to tell you something which you are not grasping. A recurring adventure dream in which an obstacle is faced but never overcome usually indicates something in you that is not being faced and dealt with. In these cases look deeply into the symbology of what you are facing in your dream.

Not all fantasy dreams are what we would call adventures. Sexual fantasies often are encountered and are easily recognized. These may be initiated for a variety of reasons. A physically unfulfilled desire for sex is an obvious cause for such fantasies. The wish to explore your sexual nature outside of the bounds of social stricture is another. If you dream of engaging in sex with a stranger or with someone for whom you have a sexual attraction in physical reality you are probably just playing out a fantasy. If, however, there is some unusual aspect to the encounter you should look into the symbology.

In dreams we also encounter situations in which sex plays a part but is not the main theme. If you dream of having sex with a parent you might be inclined to worry about the psychological ramifications, but this is not generally necessary. The mother figure is symbolic of Mother Earth, the feminine aspect of existence, the Goddess, and sex with this "mother" often symbolizes an encounter with the feminine aspects of reality, which involves intuition, emotion, and inspiration. The same sort of symbology is encountered with father images. Anytime we receive something through some aspect of reality we are in essence playing the female to the male aspects of reality.

Fantasies can take on many other forms as well. If you are poor you might dream that you are rich or living in a richly furnished setting. If you are ambitious you might dream about fame or success. We engage in such fantasies for a variety of reasons. The first, of course, is for the simple enjoyment of experimenting with situations we desire but have not encountered in physical reality.

Frequently, within the Dreamscape, we manifest our desires, inclinations, hopes, and fears in order to face and examine them. We may be wondering if we truly desire what we think we desire, and thus may be using the freedom of the Dreamscape to investigate. Therefore, though some fantasy scenarios require no deep interpretation, often on examination they will reveal clues to our personal drives and needs.

Fantasy and adventure encounters within the Dreamscape are often private creations. We use the freedom we have in the dream environment to create things easily which we find hard or inadvisable to create in the physical environment. In this level of the Dreamscape, which is nearest to the physical environment, everything takes on appearances similar to those encountered in waking reality. Sex, physical danger, wealth, and earthly power have nothing to do with the dream environment in and of itself. In dreams about such things we are using the dream environment to play with desires that relate to the physical environment. The imagery in adventures which deal specifically with the Dreamscape takes on a tone that is entirely different from what we are familiar with in waking life.

All experiences, whether in the dreaming or waking environment, partake of adventure and fantasy to some degree. If your dreams seem to be about nothing but adventure and fantasy, however, you might want to reexamine your physical waking life. A habitual resort to adventure and fantasy within the Dreamscape could indicate a critical lack of adventure, challenge, and enjoyment in your waking reality.

In recording and interpreting your Dreamscape experiences, try to put the simple elements of adventure and fantasy to one side. Determine to what degree they are encounters with challenge and fantasy, and search the symbology more deeply when they seem to diverge from this simple aspect. Then you can apply yourself to interpreting and examining the remaining elements. As always, let your intuition be your guide.

RELATING TO OTHERS IN THE DREAMSCAPE

Social interaction of some sort takes place in nearly all our dreams, but the type of interaction with which we are familiar in the waking environment is characteristic of the first stage of experiencing the Dreamscape. Even in the private creations of our personal dream experiences we are social creatures. When there is no one else with us in the dream we often manifest the image of someone to accompany us on our adventures. In interpreting dreams it is necessary to discern the relative importance of the parts played by other people in any scenario.

As Jung and other psychologists have pointed out, some of the individuals with whom we come in contact while dreaming are aspects of ourselves. Repressed or unconscious parts of our own personalities may be projected outward in the Dreamscape where they take form as other people with whom we then interact. We often use projection—in the Dreamscape and in our waking lives—to objectify portions of ourselves so we can confront them and deal with them more effectively.

In other dreams we create images of individuals with whom we are familiar, and practice interacting and socializing with these projected images. Sometimes we simply desire to see people we know and create their images in the dream environment. Or we may have unfinished business with them, and attempt to complete it in our dreams. For whatever reason, the individuals we encounter while dreaming are often self-created images and not what we normally would think of as true individuals.

However, there are cases where while dreaming we do in fact encounter other individuals who are not created by us but are independent beings. Sometimes we meet with the dream bodies of individuals we may know in physical reality. And at other times we may be fortunate enough to encounter beings who have their primary focus of existence outside the realm of physical reality. Whether the beings we meet are self-created images or independent entities, we can learn from them and our encounters.

Through meeting others in the Dreamscape we learn about relationships. Whether facing dream enemies or making love with fantasy lovers, in part of our involvement we explore the nature of our relationships with others. Even if the individuals with whom we relate are our own creations, we are still bound by the laws of responsible conduct which require that we treat others with respect and recognize their inviolable natures.

Anytime you encounter another person in the Dreamscape examine the part he or she plays. Is this person accompanying you just out of the range of sight so that you are merely aware of a presence? If this is the case, and you are aware of who it is, is it someone you know in physical reality? Or are the other individuals you encounter players in a drama, strangers who act out roles but with whom you have no close encounters? Or do they take active, creative parts in the scenario in which you are involved? As mentioned earlier, note the relative clarity with which you perceive these individuals as you record the parts they played in your dream.

Always examine your behavior toward other people in your dreams. How do you treat them, and how do they treat you? Do your dream interactions mirror the way you relate to others in physical reality, or do you see yourself relating to others in a different way? Your social interactions in dreams can tell you much about how you view others and how you wish to view them. Whenever someone else is in your dream there is some social aspect which can be examined and from which you can learn about how you deal with other beings.

In many cases, in this first dimension of the Dreamscape the individuals you encounter assume one of two positions: either they are accompanying you and sharing your adventures or they are players in the drama that is unfolding. If they are players in a scenario you should pay more attention to your inter-relationships, because the dramas you encounter are often lessons depicted in a scenario of action. Sometimes the people represent something other than actual individuals, such as human qualities or archetypal energies. Or, they may embody character types that we naturally encounter in our lives. If you have difficulty dealing with aggressive people in physical reality, for example, you may repeatedly encounter aggressive people in your dreams in order to practice relating with such types.

Any dream experience can be broken into its component parts, although ultimately it should be viewed as a whole. But by taking it apart you often can get more out of it. Sooner or later you will meet all kinds of people in dreams, most of whom will be strangers to you from a physical reality perspective. Attempt to separate the social interactions from the drama of the dream and analyze or interpret the social components. Learn what you can from watching the way you deal with others in your dream setting.

In the Dreamscape you often will find yourself experimenting with social behavior. You may even find yourself doing things you would never do or behaving towards others in ways untypical of your waking life. You may dream of confronting your boss and telling him or her that you believe you are being treated unfairly, whereas in physical reality you are afraid to do such a thing. Or you may find yourself talking pleasantly with someone with whom you have an antagonistic relationship in physical reality. You can use the freedom of the Dreamscape in a variety

of ways to experiment with methods of social interaction. Try to discern the motivations for your behavior during all dreaming encounters and use the
insights gained to improve your relationships with
others in waking reality.

Inevitably you will encounter individuals who are
more adept at operating within the Dreamscape than
you are. It is important that you learn to recognize
these situations because they nearly always involve
valuable lessons. You might meet with a personal
teacher in the Dreamscape, and I will discuss this
possibility further in Chapter Ten. Or you may so-
cialize with an individual who has more experience
in the nonphysical realms, just as you would talk to
someone in physical reality who has more experience
than you in some area in which you have an interest.
In either case, pay close attention to such encounters;
we can always benefit from the wisdom of others.

In some instances you may be allowed to participate in someone else's dream. Just as you might invite
a friend along for an outing in physical reality, someone you know may invite you along for an outing
within the Dreamscape. You could see some of the
dream creations of this other individual, just as in
physical reality you could hear a song or see a painting that was created by another person. Or you might
experience elements of the Dreamscape with which
your companion is familiar but which are foreign to
you. So when you are examining your dreams consider the possibility that some of what you are experiencing is created by someone else.

As explained earlier, the Dreamscape is not a totally
private realm and the entities we encounter are not
always simple illusions. Although we often engage
in private activities or in dramas that result solely
from our own desires and intents, sometimes others

in a dream participate in the creation of the dream scenario. Different kinds of beings can be encountered, and in most cases their natures will be veiled by an image to which we can relate. In recalling our dream experiences we must use our intuition to search for subtle clues as to who it is we are dealing with in any situation.

In some cases the individuals we encounter while dreaming are symbolic of something, as in the case of a mother or father figure. This is not to say, however, that someone we meet in a dream but do not recognize is necessarily a symbolic creation; he or she is just as likely to be an independent individual, as we have discussed. We have ongoing lives in the Dreamscape just as we do in the physical environment, whether or not we are aware of it. And there are many beings with whom we have dream relationships even though we do not have corresponding physical relationships with them. If you pay attention to the frequency of encounters with individuals in your dreams you can recognize those you know only in that realm, and even expand or deepen those relationships.

According to Patricia Garfield in her book *Creative Dreaming*, the Senoi, a primitive people living in the jungles of Malaysia, believe strongly in our ability to meet new friends in the Dreamscape. Kilton Stewart, an American educated in the fields of anthropology and psychoanalysis, and Herbert Noone, a British anthropologist, spent several years studying the use of dream experiences by the Senoi people. According to Garfield, who spent time with these Malaysian people and who also draws upon the works of Stewart and Noone, the Senoi encourage active dreamwork from childhood onward. The Senoi advise that friendly figures frequently will be encountered while dreaming, and that the dreamer should encourage and develop such friendships. Such dream friendships, they believe, can lead to positive and constructive interactions.

Adventures, fantasies, and social encounters are common to the dream experience, and you will come upon many of these as you recall and record more and more of your dreams. As with other aspects of the Dreamscape an increased familiarity with the types of activities in which you engage will enable you to better understand how you are using this environment. Often we will allow ourselves to confront or learn things in the Dreamscape that we are not quite ready to deal with in waking reality. Investigation, exploration, and interpretation allow us to bridge the gap and join the insights between the two realms, thereby facilitating our inner growth.

The two realms are not as separate as we have made ourselves believe. It is only through long training and habit that we have convinced ourselves that they are two distinct, disparate worlds. With increased experience in the Dreamscape you will discover that the life you lead in the dream environment is more closely connected to your life in the waking environment than you now might imagine.

Discerning and understanding your early experiences in the Dreamscape will free you to go deeper into this new territory. We cannot walk without first learning to crawl, and we cannot explore the deeper ranges of the Dreamscape, and remember these explorations, without first dealing with the simpler ways we exercise our consciousness in this other environment. As children we spent more time playing with reality and imagination than we do as adults. Likewise you will find that you are mostly playing with adventure and fantasy, with basic fears, wonders, and

hopes within the Dreamscape during your first remembered encounters. Once again, not all such adventures are self-created, but the beginning student
of dreaming most often recalls those adventures and
fantasies which he or she has created for amusement
and discovery.

If you were to consider all of your playful excur-
sions within the Dreamscape as deep psychological
encounters or as highly symbolic flights of consciousness you would be attempting to read more into them
than is necessary for understanding. You would be
obscuring the simple with superfluous complexities.
For this reason you first should learn to recognize
your own creations involving adventure, fantasy, and
social interaction—those which occur on the near
shores of the Dreamscape.

5

The Dreamer's Work: Integrating the Self

Most of the elements we recall from our activities within the Dreamscape do not involve direct exploration of that realm; they are instead memories of the ways our dreaming consciousness has been employing that environment. The dreaming aspect of our consciousness is already familiar with its natural realm and, therefore, has little interest in exploring it for the sake of discovery. It naturally goes about employing its native abilities for the betterment of the whole self.

There are aspects of your self that are more aware within the dimensions in which they operate than your waking consciousness is. Just as your waking, thinking self knows best how to function within the physical environment, your dreaming self knows best how to interact with the Dreamscape.

At first it is only through secondhand examination of the activities of your dreaming consciousness that you can discover or infer the nature of the environment in which dreams take place. Later on, after you have developed more familiarity with the Dreamscape from the perspective of waking consciousness, and after you have learned to take a bit of your waking consciousness into the Dreamscape, you will be able to pursue direct explorations of the dream environment. For now, however, you must learn more about the ways dreaming consciousness uses the Dreamscape.

THE DIFFERENT LEVELS OF THE DREAMSCAPE

Though events in the dream environment do not occur within space as we know it, the Dreamscape has a "geography" of sorts. One way of looking at it is to say that as you venture more deeply into the Dreamscape you simultaneously encounter deeper levels of your own being, levels of your consciousness which operate within and interact with the various levels of the Dreamscape. Because our waking focus of consciousness relates to reality through the parameters of space and time, we naturally translate any experiences we recall from our travels within the Dreamscape into terms that agree with our concepts of space and time.

Consider for a moment where you are now. Perhaps you are sitting in a chair reading this book. Now close your eyes and imagine that you are in some other familiar setting; visualize it clearly. In a very real sense a portion of your awareness has traveled to that other place. You may say that it is just imagination, but even so your attention has traveled away from your current physical setting into the realm of imagination. However, you have not really gone anywhere in terms of spatial orientation.

The conditions within the Dreamscape are somewhat similar to this. While in the dream environment you may be observing some self-created fantasy one moment, then, as a result of attuning your attention to deeper layers of your own being, find yourself instantaneously "transported" to a scene in which you are juggling possible courses of action. In terms of space you have not gone anywhere, but in terms of conscious focus you have traveled to another level of the Dreamscape altogether. Spatially, these two regions may permeate one another, but for all intents and purposes they are in different "places."

I recognize that this is not an easy concept to grasp, immersed as we are in a system that is ruled by the parameters of time and space. In discussing the "geography" of the Dreamscape it is necessary to employ terms derived from our concepts of reality as we know it in the physical dimension in order to convey the essence of the experiences we may have within the Dreamscape. Therefore, when I speak of the relative distance of a particular region of the dream environment from the physical environment, you might consider it as a psychological distance rather than a spatial distance. The deeper realms of the Dreamscape are farther removed from our accustomed focus of consciousness than are the nearer realms. When I talk about the "distance" which must be traveled in order to encounter these realms I refer to how deeply you must delve into your own consciousness.

Consider the region of the Dreamscape in which we deal with the events of our daily lives and with our own psychological stance in physical reality as the one nearest to the physical dimension, the first level of the Dreamscape. The second region, somewhat deeper within and farther removed from waking life, is that dimension wherein we encounter self-created adventures and fantasies. The third level is where we juggle probable or possible courses of action and is one step farther removed from our conscious orientation in physical reality. Other realms which are less involved with our private creations, which are more objective in nature, are even farther removed from our normal focus of consciousness, and therefore can be said to exist at even greater distances from our everyday world.

I believe that we are operating on all levels of being simultaneously, that our overall consciousness is active on all levels all the time. Our waking focus of consciousness is not aware of all of these operations, however, and is incapable of sustaining an awareness of all of them simultaneously. Therefore, we must "travel" through levels of our own consciousness to witness the operations of our consciousness within different layers of reality, not only operations which are purely subjective and self-created, but also those which have an independent and objectively valid existence.

DREAM INSIGHTS INTO WAKING EVENTS

The aspect of the Dreamscape that psychologists and dream researchers have studied and investigated the most is the level which involves dreams that are closely connected to events in our day-to-day lives. It is the realm of the unconscious where our dreaming relates to feelings about and attitudes toward our daily experiences. In this part of the Dreamscape we encounter repressed or alienated aspects of our own personalities, often in highly symbolic guises. Here we also may discover formerly unrecognized attitudes and feelings.

Once you have unraveled the fantasy and adventure aspects of your remembered dreams you need to begin looking into the hidden meanings behind the symbols you have encountered. It is fairly easy, while awake, to ignore those aspects of our personalities or behavior that we do not like or are somewhat afraid of facing and changing. Also, we may be operating within an erroneous framework of belief patterns about the nature of reality; we do not examine it in our waking lives because we have no idea it is mistaken. Many of these aspects, attitudes, and beliefs are faced in this second level of the dream environment, and they often appear to us in symbolic forms.

Why do we hide things from ourselves? First of all, if we face our shortcomings we may feel obliged to make changes in ourselves. It is easier to maintain our personal status quo than it is to change. So the first answer to the question is that we are lazy. Another reason might be that we are afraid of what we might find upon close self-examination. Perhaps we believe that underneath we are sinful or evil creatures. Sometimes we want to avoid the pain that might result from discovering the source of our fears. Finally, one of the main reasons for avoiding self-examination stems from insecurity and an uncertain sense of self. If we face our shortcomings we must change them, and if we change ourselves, then who are we? Often we are afraid of transcending ourselves because we believe we will lose our identities thereby.

The dreaming self is not so attached to rigid concepts of identity. Freed from the gaze of peers and the possible censure of society it knows that self-overcoming inevitably leads not to a loss of self, but to a greater sense of self and greater freedom. As Jung might say, this aspect of our consciousness serves a compensatory role: it strives to balance the whole self by dealing with those things the waking consciousness avoids.

There are a variety of levels on which this balancing of the self by the dreaming consciousness may occur. Deep-seated fears and anxieties are not the only issues the dream self handles. Let's suppose that your partner has been criticizing you for the past few days. Because you love and respect this person you may say "yes dear, you're right," in your waking life, then feel oppressed or depressed without knowing why. Certainly you don't want to criticize your loved one in turn. In your dreams, however, you may encounter a scenario in which you behave violently toward or even kill a tyrannical king. Such a scenario might symbolize the actions of this critical loved one as those of a tyrant and reveal that you are truly angry about the situation and want to put an end to your partner's tyrannical behavior. In such a way dreams can put you in touch with true feelings that you avoid in waking life.

The occurrence of such dreams can bring about constructive changes within your waking life. If you do not face your true feelings about some situation you are limiting your ability to deal with it. If you are harboring false beliefs you are operating from a false base. And if you are carrying around negative attitudes you are not only weakening yourself but you are closing yourself off to the positive aspects of life.

Correct interpretations of your experiences at this level increase your feelings of personal power, free you for effective action, and enable you to have a harmonious and fulfilling relationship to life and reality. Perhaps the battle between the "top dog" and the "underdog" as Fritz Perls called it, is going on within you. One aspect of your psyche may be a perfectionist, demanding that you do everything faultlessly, while another defeatist aspect says that you can't do anything right. In a dream scenario you might, for example, find yourself facing your father who is telling you to be good while you, the obedient child, agree with everything he says. Such a scenario might be a clue that you have adopted the "top dog" aspect from your father and that you are still behaving like the child who accepts the dictates of authority while believing that you can never measure up to authoritarian demands.

The ways in which our psychological structures and behavioral natures may be revealed to us in our dreams are as varied and complicated as we are. The point is that you must examine the symbols, images, and events within your dreams in order to determine what they are saying to you. Examine them in the light of what is going on in your life. Use your intuition to ascertain how, and if, they relate to what you are doing or experiencing in your waking existence. You will find that when you interpret a symbol in its proper light you will get a corresponding "feeling" of rightness. If your interpretation does not point you in the direction of constructive change the interpretation is either incorrect or the dream is not of the level of dreaming which relates to your waking life.

Many of the dreams at this secondary level of dreaming offer opportunities to examine your beliefs, attitudes, and feelings about your life and reality more closely. Some involve warnings, and may indicate that a course of action you are contemplating is likely to bring you more trouble than it is worth. Others may be simple reflections of your feelings or thoughts regarding something you witnessed during the day, such as a movie you saw, a book you read, or some act you observed. Others are precognitive, foreshadowing some upcoming event in your life.

The Dreamscape is a perfect realm in which to reflect upon the events of the day at leisure, while free from physical demands. In the course of the day events often follow one another so closely that you simply do not have time to examine their significance and ramifications. While dreaming you may replay some of those events, reshaping them into symbolic forms which incorporate your perspective on them. It is the natural function of the dreaming self in this region of the Dreamscape to use symbols to portray not only the object or event under consideration, but also the way you consciously or unconsciously see it or feel about it.

You should also remember that at this level of dreaming your focus of consciousness tends to wander and skip around, just as your waking focus does, lightly reviewing and encountering a multitude of different things. Dreams at this level will not always be so important that you must struggle to interpret them. Your intuition, as always, must be the guide that tells you the relative importance of any dream.

Much has already been written about this level of the Dreamscape and our activities within it, and you may find it helpful to study some of the works of other researchers. I recommend that you read some of the books on dream interpretation by C. G. Jung, Edgar Cayce, Frederick Perls, and Ann Faraday. Faraday's books in particular contain many valuable insights into this level of dreaming and include ways in which you can go about delving into your own psychological nature through the interpretation of such dreams. But remember that these researchers deal with only one aspect of the Dreamscape, that realm in which dreams are directly related to the events of current life activities. There are vast areas of the Dreamscape they have failed to recognize and have not taken into consideration.

Problem-Solving and Decision-Making in the Dreamscape

Often when we have particular problems in our lives we turn to the dreaming consciousness to help us find solutions. While embroiled in the activities of the physical realm we are frequently too closely involved with situations to see them clearly. Concerns, duties, and responsibilities, as well as worries and anxieties thread through our minds and psyches and prevent us from seeing the broader picture. By working through our problems using another aspect of our consciousness we are able in effect to remove ourselves from the situation in order to attain an overview or a detached perspective.

For example, if you encountered a situation in waking reality in which you did not act in the way you would have chosen from the vantage of a later, more detached perspective, you might engage in a dreaming experience in which the essence of the situation is reenacted. This gives you the opportunity to try different approaches. You may dream that you conduct yourself in just the same way and then examine the details more closely; or you may act differently in the dream to see how your behavior affects you and the other participants, if there are any. You might then dream about other situations in the past which contained the same patterns, situations in which you were unable to operate effectively. One physical event or situation, therefore, may initiate a series of dreams which involve you in exploring different approaches to that situation or event.

The Dreamscape allows you to juggle situations, to create them in a variety of ways in order to experiment with different paths of action. Then from the field of possibilities you are able to enact within the dream environment, you can choose the course of action most suited to your nature and purpose. Problems can be viewed from a number of different angles. If your problem lies, for example, in dealing with a particular individual, you can stand in that person's shoes in order to see more clearly what motivates him or her. You also can look at your own problems from the point of view of another person and thereby perhaps gain insight into your own behavior and into the situations you are creating in your daily life. This dimension in which we juggle probable or possible courses of action is the third level of the Dreamscape.

Problems are not the only situations we can deal with in this way. Life is filled with the ever-present need to make decisions. Every action involves a decision on some level. We make most of these decisions with little difficulty, choosing the course that seems best to us at the time. And indeed, most decisions are of such an order that either way we go, things will work out.

Sometimes, however, there are critical junctures in our lives involving what we consider critical decisions. These may involve career moves, commitments to relationships, a change in residence, educational choices, or any number of other important matters. In these situations we are less likely to make quick choices. We want to consider the issues from every possible angle because many of these decisions involve choosing paths which will have far-reaching consequences in our lives. In order to make the best decision we naturally use every resource available to us, including the resources of our dreaming consciousness.

In the Dreamscape you are able to try out all decisions that are viable at any critical juncture. You can choose one path, then follow it to test its ramifications and your likely reactions to those ramifications. You can do this any number of times. Of course, you cannot predict all possible outcomes to any chosen path of action, but you can explore the probable consequences and how you will be likely to respond mentally and emotionally to those consequences. You do the same sort of thing in your mind in the waking environment when you must make decisions. You visualize yourself choosing one course, then imagine what the result of that choice will be. You do the same thing with other courses of action. The dreaming approach to decisions is similar but is more involved and more thorough.

Whenever you have dreams that seem to relate to decisions facing you in your waking life, examine them closely. If you make a choice in a dream, get involved with that dream scenario and see how you feel about your decision. Does it feel right to you? Do you see yourself happy or fulfilled in that situation? Look at the various elements of the dream: the tone, the symbols, the events. Take the psychological exercise that transpired in the dream and follow it through while you are awake. By doing this you are reaching into future possibilities to see what your life might be like in the event of each option. If the tone of the dream or the imagined future is unclear examine the particular symbols that arise or have arisen. Explore their meanings and associations. Do they paint a picture you like, or not? Is the scenery resulting from a course of action dark and brooding, or is it bright and cheerful? Remember that the probable outcome of a course of action, as it is displayed in the Dreamscape, is symbolically portrayed, reflecting in its imagery and symbology the mental and emotional states that you are likely to experience if you take that path.

The decision or choice, of course, is always left to your waking consciousness when the issue is specifically related to your life in the waking environment. It is our task as physical beings to deal with physical reality from its corresponding state of consciousness.

The final decision must always be made while you are awake. The Dreamscape simply allows you to pursue your options, to examine possible courses of action, and to assess various choices in relation to other considerations. If you have the opportunity to view these dreaming exercises from a waking state it is your responsibility to do so. It is also your choice whether to make full use of all your resources, of all of the insights offered by your other levels of consciousness.

In precognitive dreams, problem-solving dreams, and decision-making dreams you are probing probable sequences or events that are likely to result from your actions or choices. The future cannot be seen as if it were an already completed fact. I believe we are always free to alter our futures by what we do in the present. Therefore, whenever we encounter precognitive data in dreams we are encountering what is likely to result from the present course of actions and events. (I discuss precognitive dreams at greater length later.)

The same is true of dreams involving problems and decisions. The details of outcomes we dream about cannot be foreseen. However, because we do have fairly well established natures and we are likely to relate and react to situations according to established patterns, it is not too difficult to conceive of the possibility of "imaginatively" placing ourselves in a situation in order to see how it would affect us. By probing probable outcomes you can get a fairly good idea of the basic tone of the situation or the emotional and mental state you would adopt in any particular sequence of events.

Since we are free to choose which of the various dream scenarios we will manifest in our lives, we obviously are not dealing with any "set" future. Nor do the probable sequences we explore necessarily have to turn out the way it seems they would. At any stage in our lives we are free to change the way we deal with reality; therefore, though in dreaming we may foresee ourselves making a choice and then regretting it, we could alter our perspectives and approaches to that situation in such a way that we could make what would have been an unhappy affair into a great blessing instead. So we are dealing with probable events, not fixed, unchangeable ones. We are exploring possible futures for ourselves and, on the basis of the likely outcomes of each course of action, choosing the ones we deem most suited to our goals, purposes, and intentions in physical reality. Also, whether we know it or not, we are evaluating each possible course in terms of our nonphysical purposes, in terms of the greater purposes of our whole selves.

We are constantly weighing possible courses of action within the Dreamscape. Even while we are focused in the waking environment and going about our daily activities, a part of our consciousness is weighing and sorting through uncounted choices and possible courses of action. Perhaps you think that the choice between eating lunch at a fast-food joint or at a salad bar is an insignificant issue. The dreaming consciousness, however, knows there are important ramifications to every choice. If you go to one place you might encounter someone you would not have met otherwise. The dreaming consciousness knows many things that the waking consciousness is not in touch with, partly because it is free from the limitations of linear time. Therefore, all decisions, whether seemingly insignificant or not, involve some weighing of alternatives. Whether or not you participate consciously in that process the dreaming consciousness is involved with it.

This exploring and sorting of possible courses of actions is one of the areas in which the waking and the dreaming environments are closely connected. That aspect of your consciousness which is active in the Dreamscape at all times is in constant inner communication with your waking consciousness. Hunches, impulses, and insights frequently originate within the Dreamscape. They often are messages to the waking consciousness, nudging it in the directions most suited to its greatest fulfillment. The restrictions of linear time and physical responsibilities keep us from always having the freedom or the time to weigh every decision with all of its ramifications, and from exploring consciously all alternatives. Because of this we quite naturally delegate some tasks to the dreaming consciousness which can perform these evaluations in "no time at all" and relay the information to us through inner intuitive channels. Many times we follow the lead of our dreaming consciousness without being aware that we are doing so.

In time, with an increased cooperation between the waking and dreaming aspects of your self, you will find that you can take your waking consciousness into the Dreamscape to some degree. You will know that you are dreaming while you do so. At the same time you will be able to recall some of your waking life while you are immersed in your dreaming life. In the next chapter I go into some of these experiences in which the two realms are bridged. To know that you are dreaming while you do so yields even more freedom within the Dreamscape, for then you can consciously create your dreaming experiences. Then, in addition to the elements of your own personal dream creations you can begin to explore the objective reality of the Dreamscape itself.

6

Taking More of Your Self into the Dreamscape

If you recall many experiences within the Dreamscape you know that dreams vary in intensity and clarity and that your state of consciousness is different in different dreams. Even within the framework of a single dreaming scenario there are often elements which stand out with heightened clarity and impact while others remain indistinct or blurred. Also, within any one dream, it is possible to experience multiple shifts in the focus of consciousness.

Consciousness is ever-changing in its focus, intensity, scope, and direction. We may perceive the course of our daily awareness as running in a straight line from morning to evening within the narrow bounds of our accustomed waking reality, but in fact we jump from one dimension to another, altering our range and focus. Most of the time we are totally unaware that this is going on. A close examination of the "movements" of your consciousness throughout the day will easily reveal some of the variations in awareness you go through.

How Selective Perception Affects Dreams

By shifting attention we can turn our consciousness inward to play with daydreams, imaginings, or inner contemplations, or turn it outward to concentrate on our physical environment. Even when our attention is focused strictly on external events, there are variations in our attention and perceptions. These variations take place continually.

The intensity with which we perceive any object, event, or situation is directly proportional to the interest we have in it. If we observe something we find fascinating we invest increased energy in our relationship to that thing. We perceive it more clearly, perhaps noting subtle shades, tones, or curves. Or, if we are particularly interested in an event, we may discriminate many occurrences within its bounds. If, on the other hand, we are perceiving something in which we have little interest, we observe it only superficially, missing the details and intricacies. Therefore, our interest in a subject plays an important part in how intensely we interact with that subject.

Also, we are selective in our perceptions, magnifying those elements which interest us and diminishing those which do not, insofar as our perception of them is concerned. As we view a vast panorama, we may have particular interest in only one facet of it. By restricting or limiting our attention we allow many elements to fade into the subjective background while we bring others forward. We may concentrate so much of our attention in a narrow area that we totally fail to perceive other things that are clearly within the range of our perceptions. In effect, we invest some aspects of our environment with increased subjective reality, while diminishing the subjective reality of other aspects.

Sometimes we find ourselves so absorbed with our own inner thoughts and feelings that we are unaware of what goes on around us. Even more frequently we are so absorbed with what is going on around us that we are unaware of our own inner states. So, not only do we vary the intensity of our perception of aspects of external reality; we also turn our consciousness inward and outward, thereby changing our relationships to and perceptions of both our inner and outer realities.

As we all know, our states of mind, and emotions also influence how we relate to the reality we perceive. Our thoughts, attitudes, and beliefs act as filters. We see the world in the light of our own opinions, thereby constantly perceiving people, situations, etcetera that confirm our beliefs. And of course, our moods determine the tone of what we perceive. The world is dark or light according to the quality of darkness or light which governs our inner states. As a result of our inner conditions, our mental and emotional frameworks, we invest different aspects of our environment with varying degrees of importance. We turn away from what we disagree with and toward what we agree with.

These are but a few of the ways in which we vary the focus and clarity of our awareness throughout the day. There are many more of an increasingly subtle nature which involve turning our attention into other dimensions. These few examples, however, are enough to demonstrate the changing nature of conscious focus. They are also enough to lead us to examine how our consciousness fluctuates and moves within the Dreamscape.

Keeping these changes in consciousness in mind, look again at your experiences within the dreaming environment. The same sort of things happen there, but often in a more pronounced fashion. If, while dreaming, you become fascinated with an isolated element, other elements or images within the dream are likely to disappear altogether. You may be looking at a roomful of people, for example, and find yourself particularly attracted to one individual; as a result of your selectivity you then may find yourself face to face with that individual in a room from which all of the other people have mysteriously disappeared.

In dreaming experiences some elements or images invariably stand out more than others. This is evidenced by our selective recall of isolated aspects in a dream, as well as by the relative clarity with which those aspects are perceived. In waking reality when we enhance parts of our environment subjectively we encounter subtle variations in our sense perception as well as in our psychological perception; in dreaming reality the sensual and psychological variations are not subtle but dramatic.

Consider a dream in which you are riding in a car. You might see the car itself vividly, and perhaps the person sitting next to you. However, you may see no scenery passing by, and for all you know there may be none. Also, you may not know whether there is someone in the back seat. Your awareness within the Dreamscape can be selective to the point of excluding everything except the object on which your attention is focused.

The dramatic nature of selective perception within the Dreamscape often makes dreams appear disconnected or composed of symbols or elements that seem devoid of a context that would give them meaning and cohesion. In certain planes of the Dreamscape the backdrop is not necessary; all that is needed is the manifestation of the elements which are subjectively important to the dreamer. Our dreaming consciousness does not require the connecting fabric of a logical environment in order for the dream to yield its nature and meaning. Whether or not there are other events occurring around you within the dreaming environment, you choose what you will and will not perceive.

Your interest in isolated elements within a dream scene will pull those elements out of it, and with those elements you then will create a scenario in the context of your own interests. You will selectively hear, see, smell, feel, or taste those parts that interest you or that have an impact upon you. Once you have isolated the elements, the principle of association takes hold. Any symbol, when concentrated upon within the nearer regions of the Dreamscape, inevitably will lead to other associated symbols. While dreaming you cannot isolate an image and hold onto it. You may isolate it, but your very act of imbuing it with importance will invest it with the energy to transform into a chain of symbols adhering to your own chain of associations. This, within the Dreamscape, is the result of your selective perception.

As selectivity affects the elements within the dream scenario you are perceiving, so does it affect the clarity and intensity of your perceptions. An element you concentrate on in a dream can change in appearance quite easily from appearing dull or fuzzy to being alive with clarity, color, or power. A row of houses at one moment may be composed of identical buildings; at the next moment one particular house may become brighter, clearer, and filled with meaning. Then that one house may change in appearance so that it reflects the importance with which your selectivity has imbued it.

Every subtle change of interest, impact, or meaning you project into the elements that you are perceiving within the Dreamscape dramatically changes your perceived environment. It does not require a concentrated, conscious act of selectivity on your part; the dream environment will change easily with the subtlest of alterations in your conscious focus and intention. Your own dreaming consciousness determines the relative continuity and the rapidity of change.

As a result of this inherent mutability of the dream environment we are often at a loss to explain the rapid changes we perceive as having taken place. But this same mutability allows us to explore the changes in our own consciousness, and discover its course, and to perceive the inherent nature of the Dreamscape itself. The complexities of consciousness are such that, however much we may wish otherwise, there is a variety of ways in which events and information can be formed and organized.

VIVID DREAMS

On occasion a whole dream will take on increased clarity and intensity as a result of the focus of your consciousness. Instead of remembering isolated elements you will remember the entire dream as particularly vivid and "real." These vivid dreams are marked by the clarity with which they are perceived and recalled, and by the intensity of feeling that accompanies them.

It is common to assume that a dream of increased clarity and intensity is necessarily pregnant with meaning. After all, why was it so intense unless it was important? But this is not necessarily the case. The vividness of our perceptions in such dreams does not always lie in the meaning of their symbols, but instead may lie with the state of consciousness associated with their perception.

If on a particular day in waking reality you are energetic, your mind is particularly clear, and your emotions are high, the whole world will undoubtedly appear clearer and filled with greater vitality and meaning. However, the world has not become suddenly different and more meaningful; rather, your state of consciousness has changed in such a way as to alter your perception of the world. In the same way a vivid dream may be the result of an increased focus of awareness within the dreaming environment.

Sometimes we bring more of ourselves to bear on any situation or event within waking reality, and we do the same in the dream environment. In other words, from time to time we bring more of our consciousness into play within the Dreamscape. This may involve an increased focus of the dreaming consciousness, or it may happen because we have brought other aspects of our consciousness into the picture, aspects which are not normally applied within the Dreamscape. Particularly if you are working at being more aware of your dreaming experiences you may find yourself carrying some of your waking consciousness over into the dreaming environment. In some such instances this will result in the perception of a vivid dream.

It is also possible that a particularly clear dream does hold significant meaning. But whether it does or not, the perceived clarity and intensity afford you with the opportunity to examine the dream environment in a new light. Vivid images are easier to examine than indistinct ones are. Your intuition, or inner senses, as always, must be used to determine whether the clarity was due to the deeper meaning of the dream or an alteration in consciousness. In either case, make use of the opportunity to explore both the Dreamscape and your own consciousness further; they are inextricably linked.

LUCID DREAMS

If we take the concept of the vivid dream a step further we encounter what has traditionally been called a lucid dream. According to Stephen LaBerge in *Lu-*

cid *Dreaming,* we owe the term "lucid dream" to a
Dutch psychiatrist and author named Frederik Wil-
lems van Eeden, one of the first to do serious research
on this phenomenon. When you have lucid dreams
one of two things may be occurring. Either you have
managed to take enough of your waking consciousness into the Dreamscape for you to realize you are
dreaming, or your dreaming consciousness becomes
momentarily more aware of its link to another aspect
of consciousness—the waking consciousness with
which you ordinarily identify.

Lucid dreams are unmistakable. In them you know
that you are in the dreaming environment, that you
are not operating in physical reality. You may not
recall anything about your waking life at the time, or
you may vaguely recall some aspects of it. In either
case you know that you are in a dimension other than
your waking reality. This, in my opinion, validates
the objective existence of the Dreamscape more than
does any other dreaming experience. Usually the
Dreamscape so effectively engages our consciousness
that we seldom step back and become self-aware or
self-reflective while we are in it. Since the Dreamscape is often so closely tied to our consciousness,
and since it so effectively unfolds every subtle change
in our state of consciousness, we are naturally absorbed in everything that goes on. But there are occasions when we become somewhat self-aware; we
know where we are and we are able to reflect upon
our situation.

Stephen LaBerge has done some fascinating research into these types of dreams. Working from the
discovery that during REM sleep the eyes move in
the direction in which the dreamer is looking, he and
his colleagues had dreamers signal when they were
engaged in lucid dreams by moving their eyes in a

preestablished pattern. Using this same technique LaBerge and his associates were able to test the effects of various dreaming activities on the physical body. Oddly enough, however, LaBerge has not judged lucid dreams as evidence for the objective reality of the Dreamscape, though he expects future experiments with shared lucid dreams to throw light on this concept.

When a lucid dream occurs, at first you probably will find it difficult to maintain or hold the particular stance of consciousness that is involved in the experience. I have found that the early tendency is to get caught up again quickly in some element or event within the Dreamscape and to forget yourself as existing in the waking dimension also. When this happens you slide back into the normal dreaming consciousness and go on with your dreams.

Lucid dreams can—and I feel should—be encouraged through presleep suggestions. This is similar to suggesting to yourself that you will remember your dreams, only in reverse. You must suggest to yourself that you will "come awake" within the context of a dream. Regular and repeated suggestions are necessary because you are sending messages to your dreaming consciousness. Just as you do not always hear the messages your dreaming consciousness conveys to you in waking reality, so the dreaming consciousness must be called upon time and time again before it "hears" the message. Of course, in all cases you are talking to yourself, but you are attempting to open lines of communication between different aspects of yourself.

One of the great benefits of lucid dreaming is that, if you can sustain the state long enough, you can consciously create your own dreaming experiences within those regions of the Dreamscape where this is the primary function. If you take it a step further you can go anywhere that you intend; you can begin the real exploration of the wonders of the Dreamscape and roam through the various levels and realms which serve other functions than that of self-expression. The problem, of course, is that if you are interested enough in something to want to create it, upon its creation you are likely to get so involved in it that you forget you created it. And if you are highly desirous of visiting some objective dimension of the Dreamscape, on encountering it you may again become so absorbed in your activities you forget where you are. As with everything, practice will increase your effectiveness.

Another benefit of lucid dreams is that they allow a portion of your waking consciousness to participate in the dream environment. At these moments the dreaming and waking aspects of consciousness are very close and can share perspectives. This gives you the opportunity to significantly accelerate the process of coming to understand the Dreamscape and your own dreams. Even short moments of "awakeness" in the dream setting are valuable. Such experiences also give you confidence and encouragement in your explorations.

Another benefit is that if you are lucid within the Dreamscape you will be better able to observe and understand those usually unconscious processes that are typically enacted within the dream environment. These are of a wide and varied nature and include such things as integrating, assimilating, and comparing belief systems. They also can involve reconciling contradictory aspects of your own personality. To be lucid while these things are going on and to face them from such a perspective is to make the unconscious processes part of conscious awareness.

Finally, it should be obvious that any experience is heightened if you bring an increased awareness to bear upon it. Our goal here is to be aware of what we are doing and to do it with conscious purpose rather than to do it blindly. Even in the waking environment we have to remind ourselves of who we are from time to time. Remember, however, that we should not hold too strongly to our opinions of who we are in any given setting, for we are always more than what we think we are.

OUT-OF-BODY EXPERIENCES

Another shift in the consciousness within the Dreamscape may involve you in an out-of-body experience (OBE). The nature and validity of out-of-body experiences have been researched much more extensively than lucid dreams have; unfortunately, however, this research has been less conclusive. Researchers in this area generally look at experiences wherein subjects find themselves in nonphysical bodies traveling through what appears to be the physical environment.

In *Out-of-Body Experiences—A Handbook* by Janet Lee Mitchell we read that surveys by Celia Green at two British universities, Hornell Hart at Duke University, and Charles Tart indicated that approximately one-third of the people surveyed reported having experienced OBEs. The first psychophysiological tests of subjects reporting OBEs was done by Charles Tart. He worked with Robert Monroe, author of *Journeys Out of the Body* and *Far Journeys,* and with other subjects. These tests essentially involved recording information about brain wave activity and various bodily systems during OBEs.

The American Society for Psychical Research has also done extensive research into this phenomenon, as have many individuals around the world. For the most part attempts to verify the validity of OBEs have consisted of efforts to have the subject affect the physical world while having an OBE. In my opinion, this takes a very narrow approach to the phenomenon. It involves, once again, holding the physical realm up as the only standard by which to judge objective reality. Furthermore, as mentioned earlier, such methods have yielded no conclusive results.

Individuals who have experienced OBEs have little doubt as to their reality. From Ingo Swann, who had OBEs since he was eight years old and has been the subject of extensive studies with the American Society for Psychical Research, to anyone who has had at least one OBE, there is much agreement about the reality of the phenomenon. Perhaps the real question is not whether out-of-body experiences are real. Perhaps it is: What is the nature of their reality?

In my opinion all experiences encountered within the Dreamscape can rightfully be called OBEs. When we are dreaming, of course, we are not employing our physical bodies for our travels; instead, we are perceiving various dimensions of reality while we are focused in a nonphysical form. We are functioning through bodies that are composed of energy, but not the same order of energy that composes the physical form. This is, once again, the dream body, the spirit body of the shamans, or the subtle body, as discussed in Chapter Five. In this nonphysical form we may venture into many different regions of the nonphysical environment I call the Dreamscape.

One way of experiencing the Dreamscape while we are in this dreaming body involves a slightly prephysical version of physical reality. For the most part what we perceive in this particular nonphysical locale is an exact replica of the physical world—the world, if you will, just prior to its physical materialization. When we experience this, we can see what is occurring in physical reality, though we cannot affect it. We can speak, but we will not be heard by those we see; we ourselves can move, but we cannot move the objects we see. Many people who have gone through near-death experiences report similar perception and limitations.

When we become self-aware during an excursion to this region of the Dreamscape, and when we recall the experience after it is completed, we have been involved in what traditionally is called an OBE.

If you find yourself having an OBE on this level that reveals the physical world, there are a few things you should remember. First, it is not uncommon for the traveler to interpose self-created images onto or within the scenery that is being perceived. You may find a new feature in a familiar locale. On one occasion, for example, I traveled to my kitchen and saw a door that led into the basement; however, I knew that I did not have a basement. When discrepancies like this occur, I suggest taking a moment to "will away" or "intend away" everything that you see. Self-created images will disappear; those images which are part of the objective environment will remain.

After such an experience I recommend taking the time to examine and interpret those elements or images which were not part of the objective scenario. I could easily interpret the basement door I saw as representing a door into the unconscious. If it had been my intention at the time I could have entered this door and likely had some valuable experiences involving deeper layers of the unconscious. However, if I had entered that door I probably would have been engaging another experience altogether and would have left behind the original OBE in which I was visiting the dimension that revealed the physical world.

So another thing to remember is that during a visit to this region you will not necessarily remain there. For whatever reason, you may turn your conscious focus in another direction and thereby travel immediately into another realm of the Dreamscape. Perhaps you will move from perceiving the physical environment straight into a subjective dream scenario, or you may move into another level where you are able to perceive the spirit "entities" that dwell within all physical objects. As I see it, whenever you are in the Dreamscape you are having an OBE, and there is no reason to restrict your travels unless your intent is to concentrate your explorations within one particular area.

Do not insist or expect that your state of consciousness during your travels in the Dreamscape will be the same as that of your waking self. Though you may be thoroughly self-aware, you usually won't find, for example, that you are very analytical in your approach to your experiences. As I've said before, your consciousness is multidimensional. As a result, the state of consciousness you experience in each dimension or realm will differ somewhat from all others. Different forms of perception are involved. Different senses of self exist, for in the Dreamscape you are more free to recognize your essential unity with everything that you experience. The earth-focused state of consciousness deals with physical reality, and there is no reason to expect that you will maintain that state of consciousness while you are having an OBE, or while you are engaged in any other experience within the Dreamscape.

THE CONTINUITY OF MULTIDIMENSIONAL CONSCIOUSNESS

As should be evident by now, difficulties are encountered in any attempt to categorize states of consciousness. All the aspects of consciousness naturally run into one another. The seeming divisions are often handy, but are just as often arbitrary. We are simply consciousness focused in various directions. When our attention is attuned to one focus we perceive physical reality. When it is attuned to another focus we perceive dreaming reality, or some portion of it. You could think of this as being like tuning a radio to a particular channel; you only hear the station you are tuned into, though there are other stations giving off signals simultaneously. If we choose we can attune our perceptions to what we would consider even more foreign dimensions.

That aspect of our consciousness which is engaged in the perception of physical reality is necessarily narrowly focused. The earth-oriented intellect is not adapted to handle the variety and quantity of information to which the full range of consciousness is privy. It is oriented to deal with physical reality and to enable us to operate effectively in that arena. Therefore, many of the experiences encountered by our consciousness are filtered out or ignored by the intellect because it does not recognize them as being important or as fitting into its conception of the nature of reality.

In the Dreamscape our consciousness is much more free to handle the variety of other-dimensional experiences which are available. The sense of self is less rigid and we are less concerned about forgetting who and what we are. In that environment we are more aware of our multidimensional nature and are more willing to turn our consciousness in other directions. Therefore, by going deeper and deeper into what I have called the Dreamscape, we in essence are going further away from what we commonly have considered to be the realm of dreams, even though basically the same focus of consciousness is involved.

Private dreams are but one step into a dimension in which consciousness has a much wider field of activity. If we consider private dreams to be but one operation of consciousness we can more easily discuss further operations of consciousness in that environment in which dreaming takes place.

Our consciousness is continuous; the apparent divisions between various focuses serve merely to allow each aspect to pursue its tasks and purposes without being confused by the varying orders of different realms, just as the different radio frequencies enable many stations to broadcast at the same time without interfering with each other. When we cross the line that separates one aspect from another we are passing through an inner doorway. Imagination is a doorway into private dreams. Private dreams are a doorway into public dreams. And public dreams are a doorway into other dimensions. But these divisions and doorways do not exist for the greater self which is capable of encompassing in its view all of its multifarious aspects, and in time we will surely attune ourselves to that greater, more encompassing perspective. For the present we must have these divisions so the earth-focused aspect of consciousness will not be overwhelmed.

When we explore the Dreamscape we inevitably must explore the nature and the reaches of our own consciousness. Likewise, when we explore the reaches of our own consciousness we are exploring the reaches of reality itself. It is only because we are examining nonphysically focused aspects of awareness from the perspective of our consciousness as it is focused in physical reality that we must consider them to be of other realms. From the perspective of the greater self there is but one realm with many facets, and each facet requires us to employ a unique form of perception. It is our task to assimilate, as much as possible, the perspective of the greater self so that we may become more fully who and what we are.

7

Experiences of the Transcendent Self

Explorations into the deeper regions of the Dreamscape inevitably lead us into more sublime encounters with the nature of our own consciousness. On the outer edges of the Dreamscape, where we enact private dreams, we indirectly deal with our own consciousness by viewing scenarios which manifest aspects of our own psyches. But, as should be clear by now, the earth-oriented personality is not the only focus of our consciousness. Furthermore, the earth-oriented personality with which we now identify is not the only personality available to us.

I think of the greater self as a ray of white light shot into the universe. As it strikes the "atmosphere" of the universe it is refracted into numerous component parts. Some of these now isolated rays become various earth personalities: one may be a man living in the twelfth century, another a woman in the sixteenth, another a man in the twentieth, and so on. One such ray could be seen as your dreaming consciousness. Other rays involve focusing greater consciousness into other dimensions of existence altogether.

Within the dream environment these various focuses of consciousness may meet, interact, or merge. One ray—the one with which you most identify— may alter its frequency of perception and partake of the experiences of any other focus. You may become one of your other aspects, thereby knowing yourself in one of your other manifestations. Each of these focusings of consciousness sees itself as the core consciousness; but each must develop an awareness of all the others. Eventually, as each focus accomplishes its particular purpose, all must merge into the one greater, more encompassing light, so that all returns to that fuller perspective.

MULTIPLE PERSPECTIVES AND PERSONALITIES THROUGH TIME

Let's look at some of the ways in which we may encounter other aspects of our wider natures. To begin with, whenever we engage in studying and interpreting our dreaming experiences we are already engaged in attuning ourselves to another focus of our consciousness. Our waking and our dreaming consciousnesses are distinctly separate as we encounter them, but at the same time they are merely different focuses of the same consciousness. Our consciousness is quite able to focus simultaneously not only in different dimensions, but also in different times, and it is able to form new configurations of consciousness. In lucid dreams, for example, we are simply allowing two different focusings of our consciousness, the waking and the dreaming, to overlap temporarily, thereby creating a new arrangement of our consciousness.

I feel it is important to understand these interplays from at least two different perspectives. From the perspective of your consciousness immersed in linear time your waking awareness is the only consciousness, though you may focus in other directions and perceive the Dreamscape or maybe an experience from another lifetime. From the perspective of your greater consciousness, however, free as it is from the limitations of time, space, and physical dimension, you are entertaining multiple perspectives and personalities which constantly interact outside of the framework of time.

REINCARNATION AND PAST-LIFE DREAM EXPERIENCES

The concept of reincarnation or transmigration is so old that we do not know its origins. Buddhist and Brahmanical doctrines propound it as a fundamental principle of reality. In the Egyptian *Books of Hermes* it is said that "The Soul passeth from form to form. . . ." There is reference to reincarnation in some of the works from the tradition of Judaism, and in the Koran it is stated that "God generates beings, and sends them back over and over again, till they return to Him." References to this concept in religions and philosophies are abundant, and proponents of this theory over the ages have included such thinkers as Goethe, Schopenhauer, Benjamin Franklin, Emerson, Thoreau, and Yeats.

Dr. Ian Stevenson, psychiatrist and former chairman of the Department of Psychiatry at the University of Virginia School of Medicine, has written several books that offer strong evidence in support of the theory of reincarnation. Stevenson investigated hundreds of cases in which individuals seemed to remember past lives. He concluded that "reincarnation becomes a very serious contender as the most plausible explanation of the empirical facts" as we read in *Reincarnation—An East West Anthology*, compiled and edited by Joseph Head and S. L. Cranston.

Massive as the body of evidence is in support of the theory of reincarnation, nothing conclusive has been determined. It is left, therefore, to individuals, as in so many other cases, to determine for themselves whether to believe in this phenomenon and whether to seek their own evidence. Personally, I have been convinced of the reasonableness of the doctrine. As a result, I have sought my own evidence and have encountered enough experiences I feel came from my own past lives to confirm my belief. If you want to seek your own "proof," one of the best places to look is in the Dreamscape. But it is hard to distinguish between symbolic dreams that concern this life and true past-life memories.

As stated previously, within the Dreamscape time is not linear. Instead, action often takes place in what might be termed the infinite present. Those experiences we have had, or more properly, do have, in the past are as easily accessible to the dreaming consciousness as are those we consider to be in the present. Past, present, and future only have meaning in the context of linear time. It is as if our earth experiences were on a roll of film. The dreaming consciousness does not have to sit and wait to watch the isolated scenes roll by in sequence, one after another; it has access to the whole roll and can view any portion of it whenever it is appropriate.

This concept of the experience of the simultaneity of time is perhaps the hardest for us to grasp, immersed as we are in the realm of linear time with our intellects geared to interpret reality as a sequence of occurrences. Attempting to discuss it can be even more difficult, as our language is also designed from a linear perspective. It is one of those things which must be experienced, and even then bringing the experience home to the waking consciousness can be tricky. However, I know of no better way to experience the simultaneity of time than to venture deeply into the Dreamscape.

Because our dreaming consciousness is independent of time, our other incarnations and the experiences contained within them are more easily observed by this aspect of our consciousness. For this reason you sometimes have dreams in which you view activities originating in a past life. These are not always so easy to recognize, partially because any recollection we retain on awakening will be viewed through the filter of our waking concepts of reality and in conjunction with our waking sense of identity.

However, there are clues to the possible encountering of experiences from another time. The most obvious is the perceived setting. Civilization takes on a different face in every time period. Architecture, clothing, modes of transportation, household implements, and technology are all different at each age in history. If your dream is set in a house lighted by a lantern or candle, where cooking is done over a fire, you may suspect that the time period is different from the present. Obviously, if there are horse-drawn carriages in the streets and everyone seems to be wearing clothing we associate with George Washington, then this can be a clue that the dream might involve a setting from a past life. Of course, these things encountered in a dream scenario may not be associated with a past life; but it is also possible that they are connected.

If in a dream you are reliving a past—life experience you, of course, will be enacting a different personality. This might be hard to recognize at first glance since we rarely pay attention in dreams to our own personalities or appearances. But if on examination you find that you were behaving in a manner uncharacteristic of your present personality, this could be another clue. Most likely, your drives, interests, values, and purposes would have been different in a different incarnation. Your sex may have been different, along with your position in society. Of course, any single clue such as these must be interpreted and examined in light of the other elements of the dream, such as its setting and tone.

You also would expect the spoken language in a past-life experience to be different. However, I have come to believe that our perceptions in the Dreamscape often involve telepathic communications. How often in a dream setting, after all, have you seen another person's lips moving? Communication in the dream environment is usually nearly instantaneous, and there is no language barrier. But if you do perceive that another language is being spoken in your dream, you could take this as a clue as well.

We cannot always use the familiarity of the individuals we encounter as an indicator of past-life dreams. You may have shared past–life experiences with individuals with whom you are now familiar. They would have looked different then, of course. But in translating the dream experience into waking consciousness it is quite easy to place the familiar face on someone you know. Therefore, even though you see people in your dream whom you recognize now, it does not rule out the possibility that you were involved in a past–life experience. It is only natural to envision people in the guise by which you know them now; after all, the dreaming consciousness is not attached to the stability of physical form or appearance.

Finally, any clues to past–life experiences which you have obtained in the waking perspective should be used for possible correlation. Perhaps you have always had an affinity for a particular country at a particular time in history. Perhaps you feel you have strong but latent abilities or talents; you may have manifested these in another life. Or perhaps you have an affinity for a particular foreign language. If you can establish some connection between other evidence relating to a past life and a dream in which you have encountered past–life experiences, then you are a step ahead in your interpretations.

Even when I was quite young I had an affinity for nineteenth-century Russia, for its literature and history. In reading Russian literature I always found that it was easy to remember and pronounce Russian names, whereas I've always had difficulty with French names even though I've studied the language. The settings, land, and people of Russia have always seemed familiar to me. Later in life I began to get images of myself in Russia; I had dreams in which I found myself there. When I married I discovered that my wife felt she, too, had lived in nineteenth-century Russia, and that she remembers me, although we did not have a close relationship in that lifetime. Pursuing these various leads has prompted me to recall more and more of that incarnation over the years, and I am now convinced that I lived another incarnation in nineteenth-century Russia.

Whenever you are investigating indicators of past lives, appeal to your intuition and inner senses. There are aspects of your consciousness which are already fully aware of all of your earthly experiences, and these may communicate to you through your intuition. Trust your feelings and impulses. You won't be able to delve very far into the reaches of your consciousness if you dismiss the subtle clues and insights which an active intuition can offer.

REALMS FURTHER REMOVED FROM THE FAMILIAR

As I have stated already, your consciousness is involved in many different dimensions of existence.

Some of these are totally alien to any reality with which we are now familiar. There are stages of experience in the Dreamscape in which no form whatsoever exists, levels where reality is organized on totally different principles. As you pursue your exploration of the dream environment you will likely have dreams in which some of these dimensions are encountered and at least vaguely recalled.

In a dream scenario you may find yourself totally immersed in ranges, tones, and hues of feeling and energy. Waves of emotion or subtler feelings may roll over you, leaving no visual impression but still affecting you deeply. Or you might be surrounded by strange and fascinating sounds or music of an unearthly character. Perhaps you will experience a realm in which colors are felt and sounds are seen. These types of experiences often indicate that your consciousness has ventured into dimensions of reality which, though totally alien, are nevertheless just as valid as any dimension with which we are familiar.

I can say very little about interpreting such experiences. My advice is to attempt to get what you can from them. Let your waking consciousness float around the memory of such experiences. At the very least opening to new realities is a good exercise in stretching your waking consciousness. Hopefully in time we can come to understand better what such experiences hold for us.

In yet another encounter with aspects of your own consciousness, you may momentarily merge with your greater self. Freed from the narrow perspective of earth-life, our consciousness is better able to rise to wider perspectives. Such an encounter will leave you renewed and revitalized. The memory of such an experience can take many forms. Feelings of exaltation and bliss are common in such cases. Seeing the workings of reality more clearly than ever before can be an expected result of such a temporary union. At the very least you probably will remember that you had a dream that brought you a feeling of being filled with greater purpose. In some cases you may remember yourself as having come face to face with a godlike being who radiated light. It is not uncommon to be awestruck on touching the immensity of our greater selves, nor is it uncommon to envision the greater self as a godlike being.

You might encounter realms where you meet with the traditional creatures of "mythology." Here you may experience the vital spirits of trees, rivers, stones, and fire. Each object or organism with which you are familiar on earth may present itself as a living, conscious being. In such a realm, which is part of what has been called the astral plane, you can learn much about and from the consciousness that is inherent in all things.

As we explore the Dreamscape we also are learning to deal with other aspects of our own consciousness. The same is true, of course, in any exploration of the more familiar reality. As our consciousness interacts with reality, we must deal with the relationship. Our understanding will be limited to our level of awareness, but we can always transcend our limitations.

Fear is the greatest obstacle in any exploration of the unknown. It is true that new and strange experiences may change our sense of self, but this need not be frightening. If we can release a rigid sense of our own identity and our fear of changing ourselves, then exploring something new can be exhilarating and growth-producing. Reality always nurtures us and strives to contribute to our growth; it never fights us unless we face it in fear or antagonism.

DIFFERENT DOORWAYS INTO THE DREAMSCAPE

Going to sleep is not the only method of entering the Dreamscape; neither is it the only method of exploring the nature of consciousness. There are various other pathways into the inner realms, and the serious explorer should consider making use of them. Some of the methods involved in these other doorways are more difficult and some easier than exploring your dreams.

Imagination

The imagination is often considered to be a process of enacting fantasies, and nothing else. But I believe it is far more than that. When we use our imaginations we activate inner processes of visualization. We turn our focus of attention inward and create scenarios; once this is done another inner activity often takes over.

If you close your eyes, imagine a scene, and concentrate on it, the scene does not remain static. Inevitably other images follow. A sequence of scenarios can be viewed in such a manner almost endlessly. But are you consciously creating all these images? No. You may have started the process, but the principle of association quickly involves you in often unexpected dramas. This process is similar to that which is involved in the more subjective aspects of dreaming.

The imagination entertains us and provides us with enjoyment, but it also leads into other things. Its employment is an invitation to the inner self to communicate images and ideas. Imagination is an inner pathway not only to the Dreamscape, but to other realms in which consciousness is active. Aside from daydreaming the imagination can be used to discover or explore things. You can suggest to yourself, for example, that you wish to delve into your past lives. Simply make the suggestion, close your eyes, and watch to see what images come to you. Generally, you cannot predict what will come into your mind, and the images won't always be the ones you sought. In any case they can be informative, and with practice they will come to accord with your suggestions.

In these types of exercises the imagination is only a starting point. It is not wise to assume that anything you imagine while you are awake is simple fantasy. There is a reason for everything. The imagination can spark creativity, or it can be used as a conduit to receive knowledge sent by other aspects of your own consciousness. It also can initiate out-of-body experiences. The imagination works both ways—it sends messages to the inner self and receives messages from the inner self.

Meditation

Meditation is another method of exploring the inner self. By simply closing your eyes and examining the workings of your mind you can learn much. You can discover what kind of programming you are giving yourself. Your own beliefs, attitudes, and desires can be witnessed at work.

Meditation has many levels, only the first of which involves you in observing your thoughts. By allowing your surface thoughts to subside or grow quiet, deeper thoughts arise. These, too, can be allowed to subside. Deeper states then can be achieved and used as a platform for venturing into other realms, or for turning the focus of your consciousness in other directions. You also can make contact with your greater self through meditation, and thus while awake achieve revitalization and renewal. Meditation essentially involves turning the focus of attention inward. There are any number of techniques to achieve this and many states that can arise. It is up to you to discover which methods work best for you and where you want to go with the experience.

Any activity that involves you in examining your own inner nature is a doorway into other realms, a method of exploring your own consciousness. Deliberately examining your own beliefs, contemplating the nature of reality, and visualizing are some techniques that can be fruitfully employed. The more approaches you take toward opening yourself to the reality of your inner self and to the discoveries of other aspects of your consciousness, the more insight and understanding you will gain. Of course, you can spread yourself too thin. I suggest you try a few different methods in order to determine what paths you can best use to aid in your explorations. And be sure to keep a record of all your findings.

Insights gained through any of these methods can be used as corroboration of your dreams. Some of the same levels you encounter in dreaming are reached through these methods. Compare the different experiences. The whole point is to come to an understanding of the ways your consciousness operates and the paths it can take. Any insights you gain through exercises employed in the waking state will only help in your exploration of the Dreamscape.

It is important to remember that in all your explorations you are engaging your attention in different aspects of consciousness. In every dimension or realm, consciousness employs a different set of perceptual tools through which to relate to that dimension. In the earth realm we have the intellect, physical body, emotions, and physical senses. These are not who you are; they are tools with which you perceive and relate to physical reality. You cannot expect them to go with you into other dimensions since they are functionally suited specifically for this dimension.

In a nonphysical realm you cannot have a physical body, nor would it be of any use to you there. Therefore, you cannot "feel" objects in a physical way. In fact, there are no "objects" in the material sense. There are often form and substance, but they are of energy, not matter. There is no physical sunlight, so visual perception must occur through different types of vision. The same holds true of all the physical senses. You cannot perceive physically in a nonphysical realm, though you have analogous senses that operate there.

The forms you perceive while dreaming in many cases will appear to be just like their physical counterparts: you may see a car, a tree, a building, or a chair. At other times you may perceive forms which correspond to nothing you know in physical reality, forms of things and beings indigenous to nonphysical reality but which are nonexistent in physical reality. You may have difficulty recalling these latter forms since your earth-oriented intellect has trouble categorizing something to which it cannot relate. Whether you perceive forms corresponding to physical objects or purely nonphysical objects, you will be perceiving energy on a level that differs radically from that which composes physical reality. In order to perceive such "objects" you will employ inner senses that register levels of energy that do not manifest physically. Some of these inner senses correspond to physical senses, and some of them do not.

When you find yourself perceiving through a whole new set of senses naturally everything will seem strange. It is not because the nonphysical realm is less "real"; it is because you are unaccustomed to perceiving in these ways. Just as when you were a child you had to learn to use your physical senses and correlate the information you gleaned through them with your mind, so in these other dimensions you must learn to use your inner senses, and to correlate the information gathered by your nonphysically attuned awareness.

Movement is also different in the Dreamscape. You do not get from one "place" to another in the Dreamscape by walking, though it may appear at times that you do so. In an out-of-body experience you will find that the usual efforts at mobility do not serve you. You must employ imagination or visualization to see where you want to be, and then you must "intend" the move; that is, you must create the intention to move to the "place" where you want to be. It may sound simple, but the next time you find yourself having a lucid dream or an OBE, just try to move around. It's tricky business until you become accustomed to the new laws of motion.

In this nonphysical realm the private self, that sense of self to which we often cling so tenaciously in physical reality and which separates us from everyone else, cannot enter many of the dimensions to which consciousness has access. As mentioned before, constant self-reflection does not take place in these dimensions because there is less sense of one entity as distinct from all others. This may lead you to feel strange about yourself in some of these realms; it may even incline you to judge some of these experiences as being less valid than your waking experiences. But this is just a prejudice of your physical identity. You are consciousness before you are a physical being, and your sense of self must expand if you want to participate in your greater depths.

It is fine, on returning to normal waking consciousness, to attempt to interpret your experiences as best you can from the framework of physical reality. But different rules apply in different dimensions, and if you try to see everything in the light of how it fits into physical reality, you will miss most of what is going on.

In the same manner, when you get the opportunity, try looking at your waking reality while you are within the Dreamscape. You may find that to the dreaming consciousness the waking self is a dream, just as the dreaming self is a dream to the waking consciousness. Simply put, do not try to see everything in terms of the reality with which you are most familiar. You are exploring new realms, and you must make room in your awareness for new ways of perceiving reality.

Part 3

8

Self-Expression in the Dreamscape

I have been discussing the experiences you might encounter within the Dreamscape in a progressive manner, beginning with those most closely allied with the events of our physical lives and with the structure of our physical personalities: fantasy, adventure, social dreams, and dreams which are involved with or related to our daily lives and attitudes towards our physical experiences. This is the most subjective level I have dealt with, the realm where we use the inherent nature of the Dreamscape to create our own scenarios.

I have suggested that a bit deeper into the Dreamscape you can engage in "trial" enactments of possible courses of action and juggle them in an attempt to choose the best direction for you in your physical life. Then I discussed that realm where past—life scenarios are encountered and different levels of your own being are met. And finally, I discussed those deeper regions of the Dreamscape where the objective reality of the dream environment becomes more obvious, and where the environment apparently is divorced from the physical environment.

I've also submitted that our focus of consciousness

and the aspect of consciousness through which we perceive during our travels in the Dreamscape play an important role in determining what we will encounter, and how we will perceive it and relate to it. Just as we can perceive the physical world from different states of consciousness, so can we perceive the Dreamscape through more than one set of "eyes." In any realm, and within the context of any experience, our personal stance has as much to do with how we perceive things as does the inherent nature of the experience or realm we are encountering.

Because of the subjective factor inherent in all that we experience I believe it would serve our purposes to take a step back and look at the dreamer. We need to look at the dreamer's position in relation to what he or she perceives, and we must examine the tools with which the dreamer operates in this strange realm. Also, it will be beneficial to examine some of the things the dreamer can do in the dream environment, some of the forms of self-expression which can be enacted within this realm that offers us so much freedom.

SUBJECTIVE EXPERIENCE IN AN OBJECTIVE REALM

Many people would contend that the highly subjective dreams we have in the near reaches of the Dreamscape take place only in our minds. But where is this place that is "in our minds"? Is the mind a closed container existing nowhere in reality? Is the mind an unreal zone containing thoughts with no substantial reality? Or is the mind a doorway, an opening within our consciousness that connects us with the interior reaches of reality?

Thoughts are composed of subtle energies. They are not packages of nothingness with a face on them;

they are the "objects" of the mental realm. They occupy mental "space" and they interact with other thoughts, attracting those of like nature and repelling those of contrary nature. They do not necessarily cease to exist when we stop "thinking" them; they simply cease to occupy a place within our private mental space. In the public regions of mental space the thoughts of others can be met, and our thoughts can go out to interact with those of others. More about the nature of these thoughts is discussed later in this chapter.

This mental space, then, blends into the Dreamscape, into other realms. This is why we go inward in order to encounter other realms instead of going "somewhere else" outside of ourselves; we encounter these regions by passing through the doorways that exist within our own consciousness. In psychological terms, the private unconscious impinges upon the collective unconscious, and the collective unconscious impinges upon other realms of reality.

Within the nearer reaches of the Dreamscape the individual consciousness forms the images and scenarios which are encountered, but always according to the principles of the objective environment in which this freedom is possible. The self-created scenarios take shape and exist within an objectively valid environment which allows wide freedom of self-expression.

In deeper regions of the Dreamscape we encounter images other than those which we have created privately. In one realm we meet not only our own created scenarios and images, but creations of other dreamers and other beings whose primary focus of consciousness is not in physical reality. On yet other levels we encounter phenomena and "scenery" which is neither self-created nor created by other traveling individuals, but which exists as it is whether there is anyone there to see it or not. There are regions where we experience the pulsating "machinery" of universal creation, and there are dimensions where we confront other reality systems which operate according to laws that are unlike anything we know in the physical world. There are "places" where time occupies space, "places" where colors have sound, and "places" where emotions have shape. There are levels where formless fields of conscious light blend and mix and merge and create. There are multitudinous regions which may be encountered, and only the nearest ones involve us in perceiving our own private creations.

For the moment let's go back to that level where we encounter our own creations and the creations of other individuals. Here we can become acquainted with some of the basics of operating within the Dreamscape. Since this is the level we most often experience, and since it is here that we unravel the psychic knots which prevent us from achieving greater self-realization and freedom, we should look at it first. Also, this is the part of the Dreamscape to which everyone has easy access.

In waking reality we recognize some of our own creations easily because we can step back and view them as existing somewhat independently of ourselves. We can view the work involved in any creation because it is played out over time: we see the structure rise as we lay board on board with our own hands. When it is completed we can walk around it, viewing it from all sides, knowing that it is fixed in form and will not change again unless we apply ourselves to reshaping it. The key to recognizing our own creations is recognizing the tools which enabled us to do the work. But it is not so easy to recognize the tools with which we work in the Dreamscape.

Part of the difficulty in comprehending the mechanics of creating our private dream images lies with the nature of time as it is encountered in the dreaming environment. In physical reality an idea takes time to coalesce and subsequently be materialized into some physical form, but in the Dreamscape ideas often are given form instantaneously—so quickly, in fact, that we are left wondering if the idea led to the form or the form led to the idea. To some degree both views are valid, because reality is not simply clay that we may shape according to our whims. All reality is invested with consciousness and, therefore, plays a part in fashioning the forms and purposes it takes on. But to stick to the matter at hand: time is experienced in a variety of ways within the Dreamscape and this effectively camouflages the interplay between creator and creation.

The other difficulty stems from the fact that within the dream environment the need for external tools is eliminated. Nothing is built with the hands. Nothing is formed through the physical process of shaping or erecting. Our consciousness is itself the primary mover, but we do have subsidiary tools with which to work. The tools with which we operate in this realm are closer to us, are indeed part of us.

Thought Forms

"Thinking" takes on a new aspect on the shores of the Dreamscape where our ideas and thoughts produce images and scenarios. It is as if each significant thought is immediately given shape, size, color, and motion by the dream environment. Here, thoughts cannot remain just ephemeral ideas that are never acted upon; what you think becomes real, is enacted, and is given form. The "materialized" thought is not always sustained indefinitely, but so long as the thought is entertained it is real within this region; it is immediately perceivable and tangible.

C. W. Leadbeater and Annie Besant, who were well-known clairvoyants able to perceive superphysical levels of being, did some interesting research in the area of the tangible nature of thoughts. They published their results in a book entitled *Thought-Forms*. They considered thought forms to be thrown-off portions of either the mental or the desire body, which are nonphysical counterparts to the physical body existing within the superphysical realms that surround us. They pointed out that each thought we entertain produces vibration and form. As they perceived it, each thought impulse gathers around itself the vitalized "matter" of the mental or astral realm which is most suited to the expression of that thought. This "matter," then, vibrates harmonically with the thought impulse itself, thereby expressing the nature of the thought.

Leadbeater and Besant believed that there are three classes of thought forms: those which take on the image of the thinker and can easily be mistaken for the dream body; those which adopt the image of some material object with which the thinker is familiar; and those which assume a form entirely their own, expressing their inherent quality through the "matter" they gather around themselves. According to these researchers, the quality of a thought determines its color, the nature of the thought determines its form, and the definiteness of the thought determines the clarity of its outline. Below I discuss my own findings in these areas.

Because we so often are dealing with the instantaneous "materializations" of our own thoughts and ideas on the shores of the Dreamscape we are immediately involved in them. It is not as though we face a scene in which we have little or no interest and are just passing through; the scene appeared because we formed it with intention. So our attention naturally is engaged immediately in what appears before us. Being so engaged we do not take the time to step back and observe what we have made; instead, we proceed with our creation of more associated images. If, perchance, we do step back from the formations of our thoughts we are likely to create other thoughts and get caught up in them so that we lose sight of what we originally stepped back to see.

Experience and intuition tell me that our thoughts shape what we see in this subjectively filled region of the Dreamscape. They form a pattern which is taken up by the dream environment itself and given form and motion. To keep our investigation as simple as possible I will confine myself for the moment to dealing with the act of creation within that realm of the Dreamscape as perceived by the individual working alone.

The particular pattern for our thoughts and their resulting scenarios is further determined by our beliefs, attitudes, and desires. The closer we are to where the Dreamscape touches upon waking reality the more our consciously held beliefs and attitudes will apply. As we venture deeper we begin to enact the beliefs and attitudes of the dreaming consciousness, which is more cognizant of what is possible within the dream environment. But if, for example, you are "thinking" about possible career choices, you will not allow yourself to think about any choice you believe to be impossible for you. Nor would you encounter another individual within the dream environment who resembles a ball of light if you firmly believe that all conscious individuals must look human.

Further developments on the scenarios which are patterned on our thoughts arise from our own mental associations. Once we view what we are thinking, further images must necessarily arise in association with that view; our projected thoughts attract thoughts of like nature. If you project the image of an individual who is threatening to you, you are more likely to put a gun in his hand than a spear, unless, of course, a spear fits into the scheme of things.

In the mechanics of private dreaming, as you dream you entertain a thought. That thought is given form and motion immediately by the dream environment along the lines of your own beliefs, wishes, desires, inclinations, attitudes, and so on. Then, if the initial thought is intense enough to sustain a full action scenario, it will take place. Otherwise the appearance of the manifestation of your thought will lead you to other thoughts and associations, which in turn will be given form and motion and substance. This, it seems to me, is the essence of the process by which we shape our private dreams; our thoughts are the shaping tools.

Our emotions or feelings also give rise to images, and in two different ways. As we project dreams by our thoughts, we color them with our emotions. I don't mean simply visual color, but also tone and mood. For example, projecting the image of a man with a gun does not necessarily entail danger. It is the fear we project into the scenario that makes the man fearsome. Fear in this case might literally color the man, making his clothing black and his eyes dark. Generally, however, when our emotions are involved in projecting images, they give the scenario its tone and mood.

Invoking

Our emotions also shape our experiences within this region of the Dreamscape through what I call "invoking." If you witness a scene that gives rise to an emotion within you, if you emotionally react to what you perceive, then you will pull new elements into the scenario. If, for instance, you find yourself walking through a dark forest and suddenly entertain fear instead of wonder, a panther may jump out at you. On an unconscious level you are still shaping that panther by associating him with a danger in the woods. But you have not shaped him according to conscious thoughts; rather you have invoked him from the Dreamscape and he has taken form in accordance with what your associations and beliefs allow.

As should be apparent, dream images are inherently neither good nor bad. They are neither fearsome nor joyful in themselves. A deep, dark forest can be seen as wondrous, magical, and pleasant, or as a place of danger. Our emotions, therefore, determine the tone or the mood that we experience in the dream scenario our thoughts have shaped. Our emotions are the paint brush with which we color in the line drawings of our thoughts.

As mentioned previously, our level of interest in any image plays a part in determining the primary and subsidiary elements of the scenario. Our interest is the spotlight with which we light the stage. We throw greater light on elements of the most interest to us, elements which engage our attention most fully, and we dim the lighting on those elements which we find less interesting. So long as we remain in any particular dream scene we selectively light various things within it according to our level of interest. Once we have selected the areas of personal importance and highlighted them, these highlighted images serve as the core around which further scenes may develop.

It is like looking at a book of pictures. Of all the pictures, you might select just one to study thoroughly. Then you would look at it more closely and begin to selectively examine specific elements within that picture. If this were in a dream you would not be limited to elements within the physical picture; you could experience living aspects of it or experience other images which arose in your mind as a result of examining that picture, just as you can mentally examine images that arise from viewing the physical picture.

Our interest, then, serves as a tool for selection and highlighting. With it we navigate through our own scenarios, selecting the courses we will take through the self-filled region of the Dreamscape by pursuing elements from the "materialization" of our own thoughts and emotions.

Sorting

Not only do we project, invoke, color, select, and highlight the elements within our dreaming experiences; we also sort them. Whether or not we consciously realize it we do have a purpose behind each scenario we enact while dreaming. We may be pursuing adventure, fantasy, solutions to a problem, or any number of other things. According to that underlying purpose we make choices about the ways in which our dreaming will unfold. This process is closely associated with that of interest and selectivity, but it goes a bit deeper.

If you are involved in the creation of an adventure, for example, you will select those elements in your creation which most stimulate you in an adventurous way. Then you will give them additional energy to develop in new and more adventurous ways. Or, if you are dealing with some problem and examining possible solutions, you will engage in this sorting process as well, on another level. You may enact several possible courses of action which you think might lead to a solution to your problem. Out of these you will select those which you deem to be most promising. You may have enacted the beginning of a course of action only to find that it is leading you down a path you refuse to take, forcing you to compromise in a way you are unwilling to do. In this case you might eliminate that course and choose to pursue some of the others more completely. In the midst of creating you sort and choose courses of dreaming. A scenario does not have to run its course to some logical conclusion; you can begin a sequence, weigh its usefulness, and then turn it in another direction, or end it altogether.

Therefore, as we create scenarios we use our underlying purposes and our deeper intentions as scales by which to weigh, select, and sort our dream creations. We hold all that we experience, as we experience it, up to the light of our purposes, and by that light we judge how much energy we are willing to channel in any direction. Purpose becomes the tool of judgment, and intention enacts that purpose.

FACTORS THAT AFFECT OUR PRIVATE CREATIONS

Not all dream experiences are as private as we might think if we look only at the way we shape our private dream lives. Scenarios can be created by more than one individual, and indeed they often are when more than one individual is involved. Most likely, another individual could not or would not step into one of your dreams and see exactly what you see. Due to the variation in the nature of "space" within the Dreamscape, which I discuss shortly, two individuals can see totally different things within the same "space."

The extreme mutability of the dream environment allows scenarios to be shared, overlapped, or viewed as a combination of sameness and difference.

In a dream you may find yourself having a conversation with two other people. You then may communicate with one of the two alone and discover that each of you had been seeing totally different images in the "place" occupied by the third individual. Or you and another individual might be walking in a dark forest; you may perceive danger all around while your companion sees only beauty. Consensus is neither called for nor necessary in the Dreamscape. It can be obtained under certain circumstances, but usually there will be significant variations in the perceptions of any two individuals within any one scenario or "space." It is as if one whole level of the Dreamscape were a giant inkblot—you interpret it according to your own projections and what your nature leads you to see. The only difference is that in the Dreamscape the "inkblot" actually changes for each observer.

Space and distance, like time, take on quite different natures within the Dreamscape. In a very real sense dreams do not take up any space in the sense of having extension. Space, as we know it, is a parameter of the physical environment and no two objects may share the same place. It is quite common, however, for an individual to enact more than one dream scenario in the same place. Scenes may be viewed as if they were each semitransparent, like layers of colored film placed one on top of the other. And distances may be traversed in "no time at all."

Because our consciousness as it operates in the dream environment is not so narrowly focused as it is in the waking environment, it is able to involve itself in more than one event at a time. Several possible courses of action can be viewed simultaneously, and when this is done your memory of the dream will seem to indicate that several events took place at the same time and in the same place. Space simply does not have the same meaning in the dream environment.

Nor does time. Have you ever noticed that a dream that covers hours or days in the Dreamscape may involve the passage of but a moment in the waking environment? How, you might ask, is this possible if time is always linear?

Time can be experienced in the dream environment in a variety of ways. For instance, you can enact events in reverse order. If you think of time as a stream, as we often do, then you normally perceive it as if you were standing in the stream and watching the water (time) flow toward you. Or, you may turn and watch it passing by. In the Dreamscape you can move with it, pass through it sideways, reverse its course, or step out of the stream altogether.

It will be highly beneficial if in your explorations of the Dreamscape you pay particular attention to any distinct perceptions of time and/or space that appear in a new way. If you allow yourself to see time and space as less fixed than they are perceived to be in physical reality, you begin to use your consciousness in new ways. Also, understanding that time and space can vary within dream experiences will enable you to interpret and understand your experiences more clearly.

Another factor to consider is that your consciousness within the Dreamscape may jump from one level to another without warning. At one moment you may be perceiving a scenario that you have created; the next moment you could be involved in something in the Dreamscape that is little affected by your thoughts or desires. There are many reasons for such jumps. Something you have created might remind you of another region of the Dreamscape and inspire you to travel there; you may have an appointment to meet with someone, and you are called away suddenly in the midst of your private creations; or your consciousness simply may wander away to explore more objective aspects of the dream environment. The point to remember is that jumps from one level to another in the Dreamscape will require interpreting the segments of the recalled scenario in different lights and from different perspectives: you don't want to interpret something as if you had created it when you haven't.

TRANSLATING DREAM EXPERIENCES INTO PHYSICAL TERMS

In all of these experiences involving differences in perception in the Dreamscape, it is necessary to recognize the processes of translation that are involved in the remembrance of dreams. As stated before, the tools of consciousness with which we function in the physical environment are not accustomed to dealing with the perceptions of the dreaming consciousness. In some cases they are not capable of doing so. The intellect has trouble categorizing things and experiences for which it has no frame of reference. The body even takes part in interpreting these experiences in its own terms.

Almost everyone occasionally experiences the apparent sensation of falling as they drift off to sleep. Obviously there is no physical falling involved. I feel that the body is interpreting nonphysical data in physical terms when this sensation occurs. Often, as we fall asleep, we leave our physical bodies and naturally enter the Dreamscape. When our consciousness is still close to the physical environment the body is in touch with the inner sensations of the consciousness departing. It can only translate data into its own terms, and to it the closest approximation to the drifting off of consciousness is the sensation of physical falling.

The body also is prone to translate other inner sensations in this manner. Usually this happens only when your consciousness is still somewhat connected to the body. While dreaming we are fairly removed from physical reality, and the body just goes about its business of maintaining the total physical organism. But especially in situations where a person is meditating or entering an altered state of consciousness the body is still attuned to the physical focus of consciousness. Under such conditions it is not uncommon to experience sensations of physical expansion or contraction, floating or falling, or even nervousness when the body doesn't quite know how to interpret the data it is receiving.

Generally you will not have to deal with these phenomena since most involvement in the Dreamscape takes place when the consciousness is separated from the body enough so that the physical body does not receive nonphysical impressions. However, if you are attempting to explore your own consciousness and to venture into nonphysical dimensions from the waking state, you may expect these things to happen. It is nothing to worry about. If the body mistakenly interprets things in such a manner that it perceives danger to itself, be assured that it will do something to attract your attention and you won't be able to proceed. However, usually such obstacles occur only when we misinterpret our physical bodies' messages and create unnecessary fear.

On a more pertinent note, the physically oriented

aspects of mind and emotion also must interpret all impressions within the context of their own relationships with reality. This process becomes quite important when we attempt to interpret our dreams. If we experience something in the dreaming environment which has no parallel in the waking environment, our waking minds cannot deal with it. In such a case the physically attuned aspect of mind either will fail to bring through any recollection of the event, or it will translate the experience into terms and symbols that approximate what occurred but are still within purely physical and recognizable parameters.

The physically oriented aspect of mind is just that: its function is to deal with and relate to physical reality. Its realm is events as they are perceived within the context of linear time and three-dimensional space. If events are not within these parameters the physically-oriented aspect of mind has no choice but to reshape the experience into some semblance of what the event would have been like if it had occurred within the physical dimension. Inevitably, the "earth-mind's" relatively narrow focus distorts dream experiences, making it necessary for us to "interpret" our dreams to understand them.

Just as I cannot describe the experience of the simultaneity of time adequately using a language that is specifically oriented along linear principles, so the earth-mind cannot entertain or fully conceive of the concept of the simultaneity of time. However, remember that the mind is capable of expansion. It can learn gradually to deal with uncommon experiences to which it is not accustomed. But you have to deliberately turn it in these other directions; left alone it will continue to relate to reality as a purely physical and mental environment. The very exercise of recalling dreams gradually orients the earth-mind to accept information from nonphysical sources. Likewise, exercising the intuition opens the mind to new forms of input. You must convince your earth-mind that there is valuable information to be gotten from other than physical sources.

The emotions basically work on the same principle. In the Dreamscape we experience feelings and energies that are different from those we perceive in waking reality. Emotion, as the word is generally used, refers specifically to feelings abiding in the "mortal breast," to which we have given the names of love, hate, sadness, joy, etcetera. But behind the specificities of emotion is the "organ" of feeling which is employed by the consciousness to register all types of feelings, not only those associated with the human, psychological condition. Many energies that have a feeling tone are more subtle and less defined than the feelings with which we are normally in touch. Therefore, like the intellect, the emotions will translate feelings that are encountered within the Dreamscape, shaping them first into familiar categories. As is true of the intellect, your earth-oriented emotions gradually can be expanded so that in time you will be able to handle and express some of the less familiar feelings you experience within the Dreamscape.

Making the effort to interpret our dreams exercises our physical faculties in new ways. It stretches the physically oriented consciousness in new directions, sending it into foreign dimensions, though tentatively at first. With time the intellect, emotions, and physically focused aspect of ego will learn that such new information does not threaten their validity or their security within reality. They will discover, in fact, that they are expanded and given greater scope as they allow themselves to receive this new information. As the physical faculties begin to open willingly to such information the intuition will be allowed to flower, and experiences from nonphysical regions will be recalled more accurately, without always being translated into physical terms. This process takes time, however. We have trained our physical faculties to ignore nonphysical data, and they have learned the lesson well. Now we must retrain them.

Until our earth-oriented focus is fully opened to the input of our other focuses of consciousness, however, it will be necessary for us to interpret our dream experiences. We must make the effort to unravel the translations; we must teach our minds how to bring through experiences from other dimensions. To do this we must uncover the hidden meanings of the symbols and images that we do recall.

9

The Language of the Dreamer: The Symbolic Nature of Dream Imagery

Everything has deeper meaning than its surface appearance would indicate. Though it is not necessary to examine the associations to every object we perceive in dreams, or to explore its symbolic nature, something can be gained by doing so. In physical reality we seldom explore the symbolic nature of the things and events that we encounter and perceive, simply because it is not necessary. In the Dreamscape, however, and especially in those dimensions in which we are involved with our private creations, it is not only beneficial but imperative that we look into the symbology of what we encounter. Perhaps as we become more attuned to our dreaming consciousness we will find that we automatically recognize the meaning of what we perceive there, but in the beginning we must engage in interpretation.

THE FUNCTION OF SYMBOLS

Within the Dreamscape symbols and images perform a variety of functions. As direct representations of our thoughts, feelings, and states of consciousness they serve primarily as forms of self-expression. Just as a creation within physical reality is an expression of a self-achieved, coalesced concept, so are the symbols we project outward in the dream environment expressions of what we have formulated within ourselves. In this mutable environment, symbols give form, substance, and motion to our inner conceptions.

Thoughts and feelings have both shape and energy, though in the physical environment these are not automatically given full manifestation. They remain within us unless we develop them and give them physical expression. In the Dreamscape, however, thoughts and feelings have an inherent reality of their own. In this realm the patterns of our inner states automatically and naturally are translated into full manifestation. This is not to say they are physically manifested, because we are not dealing with the physical realm; they are, if you will, superphysically manifested.

Another and perhaps more valid way of looking at this is to say that thoughts and feelings are always given shape, substance, and form. But unless we travel to the realm in which that shape and substance is naturally apparent, we cannot see it. In the near reaches of the Dreamscape the shapes of our thoughts are always apparent, though in physical reality their shapes are perceived only vaguely within our minds. In the physical dimension our thoughts must be physically materialized before we consider them to be fully manifest.

Symbols, as direct expressions of who we are within the dream environment, also serve as a means of communication. We communicate with others whenever we express ourselves in ways that others can perceive. Of course, it is up to them to interpret our expressions in the light of their own understanding; nevertheless, if they can see our expressions they have

participated in a communication with us. It is often
the same in physical reality: others know us by what
we do, say, and create.

The symbols with which we express ourselves also
help us communicate with ourselves. Within the context of the reality in which they are manifested symbols serve as reflections of who we are. If, in the physical world, you create a particular career for yourself
and work at that vocation for many years, this tells
you and others something about your nature. It does
not, of course, tell everything. The same principle
operates within the Dreamscape. If we project expressions of ourselves outward into symbols, images, and
dramas, then surely these ought to reveal something
about ourselves to us.

When we begin to bridge the gap between dimensions, when experiences are shared between two different focuses of consciousness, a new factor is
introduced. As we attempt to interpret our dream experiences in the light of what we know in waking
reality we are making symbols serve as forms of communication from one aspect of our own consciousness to another. They become tools for communicating
across dimensions. Our dreaming consciousness
speaks to our waking consciousness, in many cases,
through symbols.

Let us imagine that an important experience occurs
deep within the Dreamscape, perhaps involving your
relationship with yet another dimension. If you want
to partake of that experience in the waking state you
must, in a manner of speaking, bring it back through
the reaches of the dream environment. This does not
involve just one translation. Even within the Dreamscape there are different focuses of consciousness;
there are different levels to our awareness in that
realm. So on the return trip the original experience

is translated a time or two within the dream environment so that various levels of our nonphysically oriented consciousness will be able to partake of it and step it down. Once the experience has been translated into terms that can be manifested within the level of the Dreamscape "nearest" physical reality, it must be translated yet again into waking terms.

You must understand that when I speak of these stages of translation I am speaking metaphorically. The fact of the matter is that whenever any portion of our overall consciousness experiences something, all other portions experience it on their own level as well. The whole being in one way or another is affected by anything that happens on any level, and each aspect of the self's experience of the event is perceived in terms suited to its level and nature of perception. Therefore, not only are we multidimensional, our dreams are multidimensional as well.

Because our dreams are multidimensional we may recall what we perceive as a series of dreams that restate the same theme in different ways. This experience may involve the recall of a single multidimensional dream as it was enacted at various levels of our consciousness. On each level, or in each dream of the series, different symbols will express the same concepts or realizations on different levels.

Sometimes our experiences within the Dreamscape are so far removed from waking consciousness and its relationship to reality that the version we finally recall is so watered-down or distorted that it becomes virtually impossible to reconstruct the original experience. This is due in part to the limitations of our waking consciousness, but there are some experiences which as yet cannot be brought through fully. For this reason some of our dreams will elude all our efforts at interpretation.

From the standpoint of your waking consciousness you increase the exchange of information between your own various levels and focuses of consciousness as a result of your efforts at interpretation. When you try to interpret your dreams you are sending a message to your dreaming consciousness—the message that you wish to understand its experiences. You are telling it that you want to increase the flow of information between dimensions. And at the same time, you are exercising your waking consciousness, stretching it so that it will be more open to such communications. You are telling it that you want to perceive more nonphysical experience. Your efforts stimulate the flow of information from both ends.

DISCERNING THE CONTEXT OF SYMBOLS

When it comes to interpreting a particular dream or the isolated elements from a dream, there are a few more points to keep in mind. In the first place it is important that you attempt to recall and record as much of a dream as possible. The context in which symbols or images, or even the dream itself, are encountered gives valuable clues to the direction you should take in interpretation. Consider what would happen if you were to view only short glimpses of a television program. You might not be able to tell whether the few images you saw were part of a movie, a news broadcast, or a dramatic series. You would have to watch it long enough to determine the context, the nature of the total program. The same principle holds true when it comes to recollecting your dream experiences.

Remember also that one symbol or image may represent many different things, or even various levels of the same thing, depending upon the context in which it is encountered. Consider for a moment the commonly reported dream image of having your teeth fall out. This may be an indication that you have some undetected problem with your teeth and should consult a dentist. Or if you are particularly self-conscious about your appearance, and perhaps about the way your teeth in particular look, such an image could be reflecting worry over your appearance. However, teeth falling out in a dream might be a reflection of the fact that you had lied recently or spoken improperly. Each of these possibilities, and any others that might occur to you, would have to be examined in light of the context in which they appeared, and in light of your own current attitudes and situations.

Now consider the image of a snake in a dream. Such a dream frequently is interpreted as having sexual implications. Freud certainly would have seen the snake this way. But the snake can be equated with the kundalini serpent, an image for the vital energy which resides at the base of the spine and which when activated moves upward energizing the various chakras. As the kundalini rises one of the areas it energizes is the chakra associated with sex. Therefore, we have in this scenario an image which possibly represents, or which can be seen to represent, the same thing on different levels. Once again, the context of the image within the dream scenario as well as your personal conditions would have to be examined in order to determine the most constructive and apt interpretations.

Symbols are not like letters or words which carry the same meanings whether they are written on paper, wood, stone, or a computer screen. Symbols, like the environment in which they are encountered, are mutable in nature. We employ them as we might employ colors in paintings; in one painting red may convey elements of a sunset, and in another it may suggest the image of blood. It all depends upon the context in which it is placed. So if all you recall are a few, isolated images from your dream travels you are limited to exploring the possible meanings those images might convey. Intuition will help you to narrow down the choices, but without knowing the overall context in which a symbol occurred you are severely limited.

Dreams as well as symbols exist within specific contexts. Each dream not only has its own contained environment, but it also exists within a greater environment. Some dreams may be subsidiary elements of larger dreams. Others may be parts of a series of dreams. Yet others may involve you in an unusual experience of the varied nature of time: if the dream is following the stream of time backwards then you need to be aware of this to properly interpret the dream.

All of these possible variations on the context of dreams and symbols make it necessary that we bring back into our waking consciousness as much information as possible. This is one reason for recording dreams immediately upon awakening. Sometimes the isolated symbols are not as important as the tone or lighting of a dream. Sometimes the sounds carry more significance than do the forms and shapes. And sometimes the psychological texture is the critical issue.

Also remember that your recollection of dreams may involve distortion due to the way in which you recall them. Since dream experiences do not necessarily occur in a sequential order you may find yourself remembering a collection of images which you are inclined to consider as parts of one dream. It may be, however, that you are recalling a few elements from several different dreams and grouping them together in your memory. Both the occasional simultaneity of dreams and their multidimensional nature contribute to the difficulty we have in recalling them. As said before, the earth-oriented aspect of mind must organize things according to linear concepts, and when it does so it often distorts the true context of dream experiences.

Consider also that while dreaming your conscious attention wanders just as it does in waking reality. You may be enacting a particularly important dream scenario when one element within it grabs your attention. Forgetting what you were involved in initially you might find yourself creating a divergent dream scenario that has little or nothing to do with the original intent. Then you may return to the original scenario, just as when your mind wanders in waking reality you sooner or later come back to the issue at hand.

A further complication arises when we consider that the dreaming consciousness can maintain the primary scenario while it simultaneously explores tangential scenarios. The dreaming consciousness can create scenarios which spread about like the branches of a tree, entertaining myriad perspectives that allow it to view all the scenarios with varying degrees of attention. Again, it is not limited to functioning in a sequential order.

Interpreting dreams is not easy, as is obvious by now. You cannot simply take an image and say it means this or that. Only personal exploration and study will enable you to unravel the mysteries of the way your own consciousness works. For this reason no one else can fully interpret a dream for you, at least no one whose primary focus of consciousness is within the physical realm. But dream interpretation is not as difficult as it might seem when you consider all the factors and possibilities involved and the errors you could make. Your intuition is always there to light the way.

Another factor to consider is that symbols usually take on two different aspects. They represent something other than what they appear to be on the surface, but they also are themselves. A horse is a horse and within a dream it will play the part of a horse, regardless of what meanings lie behind its appearance. It might be symbolic of your animal nature, and an examination of its condition—whether it is wild or domesticated, healthy or ill, bridled or running free—may give you clues as to the condition of your health. At the same time, though, it will remain a horse within the dream scenario, and it likely will lead you to think of other things associated with horses, such as saddles, cowboys, or pastures. If, then, when a horse appears in your dream you subsequently see cowboys and Indians it doesn't necessarily mean that the cowboys and Indians require deep interpretation.

You have to make an effort to distinguish between the chain of associations that are involved with the meanings behind symbols, and the chain of associations that are involved with the simple image itself. Once again, think about how the mind works. Say, for example, that you are contemplating the music of Beethoven, trying to feel the moods behind and within it. Your mind might go off on a tangent and begin thinking about Vienna, or pianos, or people with long hair. If this occurred within a dream you would see Vienna, or the piano, or someone else with long hair, but these succeeding images would have little to do with your contemplation of the subtleties of the music. This is another reason you have to use your intuition and insight to determine the critical issue in a particular dream.

EXAMINING SYMBOLS FACE TO FACE

Some of your best opportunities to obtain a clearer understanding of how dreaming works, and of the dream environment itself, may come in the form of lucid dreams or out-of-body experiences. In a very real sense, so long as we are studying only our memories of dream experiences we are still exploring the Dreamscape secondhand. We are not able to bring our critical faculties to bear upon these experiences so long as we are not aware of what is happening while it is happening. But if you can master and maintain the peculiar stance of consciousness that is necessary for lucid dreams you can explore their nature firsthand.

Bringing about the occurrence of lucid dreams requires more effort than increasing dream recall does. It requires an added leap of consciousness; it requires relating to reality in a totally new way. You may even find that you are reluctant to make the suggestions necessary to bring about such an experience. The physically focused aspect of ego becomes somewhat insecure once it steps out of the realm in which it naturally functions, and it may respond fearfully when you suggest to it that it accompany your dreaming consciousness, even to a slight degree, into the Dreamscape. With patience and steadfastness, however, you can achieve success in the creation of such experiences.

You probably won't be able to do much with your first lucid dream. You may find yourself standing within a dream scene, aware that you are dreaming, but fully spellbound by the strangeness of it. The experience may only last for a few short moments because you tend to quickly forget where you are and become absorbed in the activities which surround you. However, even a short glimpse of the Dreamscape from the perspective of a lucid dream is a significant step. After you've done it once you will have proved to yourself its feasibility. You also will have reassured your ego that there is nothing to fear. And you certainly will have given yourself encouragement and renewed enthusiasm.

If, on finding yourself within a lucid dream, you are able to formulate the concept of holding that stance, there are things you can do to keep from getting caught up in your dreaming. Do not concentrate your focus of attention on anything in particular. Keep looking around, lightly glancing over everything in your field of vision. If you focus intensely on any one thing you are likely to get lost in it. Also, make some attempt to move if you feel up to it. You will not have a physical body that automatically knows how to move, so navigating requires a unique application of intent or will. In the Dreamscape you do not take physical steps, obviously. Instead, you must intend what you want to do. "Intending" is not so forceful as a command, but it partakes of that tone. Perhaps it is more accurate to say that you mean to do something and believe that it will take place.

Inevitably a lucid dream experience must end. Sooner or later you will return to ordinary dreaming and forget that you are in the Dreamscape. Try to notice, when this occurs, just how the transition takes place. Examine the shift in consciousness that resulted in your returning to the usual type of dreaming. Make note of whatever it was that caught your attention, and see if you can determine why it caught your attention. If you are fortunate, or if you have given the proper presleep suggestions, you will awaken shortly after your lucid dream. Then thoroughly document what happened. You certainly don't want to forget such a significant experience. And believe me, you will find it to be a significant experience.

You need to adopt a slightly different perspective when you attempt to interpret what was seen or experienced during a lucid dream. For those short moments you, in a sense, will have stepped back from your dreaming. Because of this you will have been less involved in the immediate production of your dream scenery. Most likely you will have "come awake" during the middle of a dream and found yourself viewing a segment of it. If you can recall what occurred in the dream prior to "coming awake," or after doing so, then you can interpret those elements in the normal way.

By coming awake within your dream you automatically change it. If you were creating private dreams within the Dreamscape, the scenery will become less of a direct expression of what you are doing at the moment and more of a residual environment resulting from previously initiated actions. Of course, this is not always the case. You may come awake within the setting of a group dream, or even within another dimension, though it is more likely that your early lucid dreams will involve you in momentary alertness within the context of a private dream.

Anything you can accomplish while having a lucid dream is a bonus. If you can look at other people without forgetting yourself then you can assess their relative presence. Perhaps you can ascertain whether there are other dreamers active within your range of perception, or if they are "shadow" images simply playing parts within your own dream–drama. You may even be fortunate enough to witness dream formations taking place, scenes evolving within your dream vision. If you can sustain this stance long enough you can consciously create the elements before you, at least in some cases.

From the other end of the spectrum you may come to find that while you are in your normal waking state of consciousness, while you are going about your daily activities, you occasionally are able to "peek" into the Dreamscape. As mentioned before, your dreaming consciousness is not inactive when your attention is focused within physical reality. Dreamscape activity takes place all the time. You can get glimpses of your activities in this realm while you are awake, and the imagination can lead you into the Dreamscape for short periods of time. These experiences of perceiving the dream environment while you are awake can further increase your insight into the nature of the Dreamscape.

Finally, don't forget about using the half-waking, half-sleeping state that comes upon you before you go to sleep or just after you awaken. At these times you have one foot in each dimension, so to speak, and this can give you a unique opportunity to compare the realms. Watch yourself beginning to form dream images; but if you find yourself getting too involved in them draw back a bit so that you don't go to sleep. Use your imagination at this time to consciously create dream images. You will discover that in this state your powers of visualization are greatly enhanced. If you can hold on to your "waking" consciousness you might be able to walk into the Dreamscape with your critical faculties, thereby stepping directly into a lucid dream.

When you were a child you did not automatically

know how to organize all the elements you perceived into a cohesive whole. You didn't know how to walk until you practiced it, and you couldn't understand the communications that you heard until you had learned to make the necessary associations. As a beginning explorer of the Dreamscape you cannot expect to be an adept right away. Your dreaming consciousness may be fairly proficient at what it does, but you are approaching it from the standpoint of waking consciousness, and thus, you are but a babe in a new world. Be patient with yourself and keep trying. You will learn to understand the Dreamscape just as you learned to understand the physical realm. You will understand, that is, so long as you keep working at it and keep exploring.

10

Gleaning More from Your Dream Experiences

Though the dreaming consciousness, compared to the waking consciousness, is quite at home in the Dreamscape and able to function most adequately there, it is not necessarily completely proficient at what it does. Like that part of our consciousness which is focused in physical reality, the dreaming focus of consciousness is still learning how to create and function more effectively within its native environment. It may be able to unfold scenarios and juggle probabilities naturally, but it does not necessarily know how this is achieved or why dreaming events occur as they do. Neither is it familiar with all of the other realms of the Dreamscape where the objective nature of the dream environment is more apparent. Therefore, the dreaming consciousness is participating constantly in a process of education.

DREAM-LESSONS WITHIN THE DREAMSCAPE

Frequently you will recall dreams in which your education as a dreamer is taking place. A close observation of these scenarios will do much to inform you of the nature of the Dreamscape and the ways of the dreaming focus of consciousness. They will appear in a variety of guises, but many will be recognizable through their emphasis on symbol manipulation or on the techniques of creating the dream reality. Also, you may be able to recognize them by the appearance of another individual who takes on the role of your teacher.

I know of cases in which a dreamer has seemingly made contact within the Dreamscape with a teacher or a guide. Neuropsychiatrist Shafica Karagulla in her book *Breakthrough to Creativity* writes of such experiences. In Western culture, where the dominant attitude is one of classifying all dream experiences as products of the mind or of the imagination, this phenomenon is less common. But in cultures where dreams are considered to have great importance, teachers and guides frequently are encountered by the dreamer.

The Senoi of Malaysia, discussed previously, have a highly developed system of dream control which involves confronting and conquering danger in dreams, moving toward pleasurable dream experiences, making dreams have positive outcomes, and extracting creative products from them. One of the ways these goals are achieved is through enlisting the aid of friendly figures who are encountered while dreaming. The Senoi believe that some of the friends who are met within the Dreamscape may be induced to serve the dreamer as guides. These "spirit-guides" frequently aid Senoi dreamers by telling them about such things as songs, dances, and religion. They also may instruct dreamers in methods by which they can use their dream experiences more constructively.

Shamanic cultures lay stress on teachers or guides encountered in dreams. In Native American cultures dreams are considered to be of great importance to the individual. In some cultures the dream-life is used to contact supernatural spirits. Some turn to their dreams for help and guidance in managing psychological problems or effecting physical cures. Others use them to predict the future or to learn of efficacious rituals.

Frequently American Indian dreamers encounter spirit guardians in their dreams. These guardians sometimes "adopt" the dreamers and care for their needs, somewhat as grandparents might. Such relationships between dreamers and spirit guides would likely endure throughout the individuals' lives and aid dreamers in a wide variety of ways, according to Patricia Garfield in *Creative Dreaming*. Calvin Hall, an American dream researcher, considers spirit guides offering such long-term relationships as the ultimate gesture of dream friendliness.

More recently in the West the phenomenon of channeling, in which an individual seemingly communicates with a nonphysical entity while in a dreamlike trance, has become popular. In most of these instances the entity or personality contacted instructs or guides the "channeling" individual, sometimes offering useless or misleading information, sometimes presenting valuable knowledge that was previously unavailable to the individual involved in the communication. Undoubtedly, some channeled messages come from the recipient's own unconscious, but there are cases that cannot be explained this way. It might be contended that some of the entities contacted through channeling exist or have their main focus of consciousness within the Dreamscape itself, even though the communication does not always occur while the channel is in a dreamlike state. In some cases there is evidence to indicate that the beings contacted also can be met while the channel is dreaming.

Jane Roberts, a writer who fell into channeling, is

well known for her works that she says were derived from her communications with an "energy personality essence" known as Seth. Most of her communications with Seth took place while she was in a trance. However, on occasion she reported that she met with Seth while she was dreaming. And, on more than one instance, some of her pupils also claimed to meet Seth while they were dreaming. This suggests that at least in some cases such "teachers" or "guides" contacted through channeling also can be reached while one is in the Dreamscape or that one can enter the Dreamscape while in a trance. If you accept the objective reality of the Dreamscape, then you may consider that these teachers could be independent beings with valuable guidance and instruction to offer the dreamer. On the other hand, if you deny the objective reality of the Dreamscape, then such teacher-images could be taken for symbolic representations of deeper layers of consciousness within oneself, which also may offer important guidance and instruction.

For our present purposes let us consider that learning from a teacher encountered within the Dreamscape is an objective experience, not imagination. Let us look at what might be termed "training sessions" in which the dreamer learns how to operate more effectively within the Dreamscape and how to understand better what he or she encounters there. I will discuss examples of such learning scenarios shortly. If you can recall and study dream-events of this nature, you may find they help you to become more proficient as a dreamer.

I have found that often these training sessions appear to be conducted by individuals who may or may not appear in the guise of a teacher. Sometimes it seems they adopt the image or appearance of a participant in the dreaming scenario, perhaps to camouflage their true natures. At other times they appear as teachers or wise persons with whom you are familiar in physical reality. At yet other times they may change appearance during the course of the dream, at first being recognizable as teachers, and later blending into the lesson or the dream scenario as participants.

In my experience of these encounters at least for some portion of the scenario you simply observe the happenings. During these periods your state of conscious attention will be subtly different from that normally employed in dreaming. It is obvious that, in order to participate in a lesson on dreaming, the "student" must maintain some distance from the events so as not to get caught up in them, as would naturally happen. I believe the teacher can create this condition, but probably you will not be able to tell what has made you stand back from the events you are witnessing.

One example of such a learning-dream might involve you in watching other dreamers attempt to create or alter a specific scenario. You will be observing someone else's dream, thus, you should be able to recognize your own lack of personal involvement in the events taking place. The other dreamers may be placed in a situation which contains some seeming danger; they then might be left to create a way out of that danger. You will be able to watch them get caught up in the event as they forget that it is a training session, until eventually they recognize that they can control the events surrounding them. At this point you will likely see them bring the scenario to some conclusion in which they either remember that this is just a created scenario, or they overcome the danger within the context of the dream scenario.

On other occasions you may be put in the same type of situation and be called upon to solve a "dream-riddle." In retrospect you can recognize this as a training session and not just another private dream creation if you recall one of two things about the dream: either the beginning of the dream when your initial instructions were given by the teacher, or the moment within the scenario when you "awoke" to your true situation. These types of sessions are often difficult to recognize because you usually are so involved in the dream scenario that you recall only the drama-lesson itself. You might remember the dream simply as one in which you faced some danger, for example.

Another instance of a training-dream could involve you in what appears to be a classroom setting in which several dreamers are participating. Dr. Karagulla, mentioned earlier, wrote about this situation. I have known occasions wherein the instructor created a scenario before the vision of the students as if he were projecting a movie on the wall. Then, after discussing the ongoing scenario, he invited the students, one by one, to step into the scenario and experience it directly. Such situations afford a unique opportunity for observing the changes in your focus of consciousness which are necessary for the transition from one setting to another.

Other situations involving lessons in dreaming and functioning within the Dreamscape could require dealing with symbols rather than full scenarios. You might find yourself in a dream situation that at first seems like any other dream. The difference, however, is that someone else is influencing the images you perceive, though you may never be aware of this individual's presence. You will confront symbols and images that are not the result of your own concep-

tions and feelings, but which instead serve to stimulate conceptions and feelings in you. In a way it will
be as if you are being manipulated or tricked into
believing something. For example, you may walk into
a house and notice that the floor is blood-red in color.
Then you might see a gun lying on a table. The atmosphere or psychological tone of the interior of the
house may feel strange, as if something is wrong;
what you see could even be visually distorted. Finally, you may catch a glimpse of someone whom
you recognize to be an actor who plays the part of a
television detective. All of these things could lead
you to believe that some crime has been committed,
and you subsequently might proceed to try to solve
the crime. Eventually, in the course of your investigations you may discover that there was in fact no
crime and that someone set things up in such a way
as to lead you to false conclusions. You may even
learn that the "detective" you saw was a teacher playing a part in his or her own teaching-drama. This is
an example of a case in which you were being shown
how your own interpretation of symbols and images
leads you to perceive things through the framework
of your own attitudes and feelings.

Some dreams are not necessarily planned as learning situations, but nevertheless serve that purpose.
Most of us have experienced the dream situation
wherein you decide that you don't want to experience
the dream events anymore. Subsequently the dream
ends or changes. In these occurrences you have a
slight recognition, from the standpoint of dreaming
consciousness, that you create some of your own
dreaming experiences. This recognition sometimes
allows you to alter your dreams consciously.

This ability can be extended. For example, you
might achieve a state of semilucid dreaming which

is not a fully lucid dream, but one in which you are still vaguely aware that something is different. Your waking consciousness is entering slightly into the Dreamscape. Perhaps you pause long enough within the context of your dreaming to look around and wonder about your location. Or you might vaguely recall your waking life in the midst of a dream, thereby causing you to reflect upon the apparent differences between your waking existence and your dreaming experiences. How far this change of perspective progresses depends upon your level of development. It could even unfold into a fully lucid dream.

You might have experienced flying dreams, dreams in which you soar "bodily" through the Dreamscape. These are important because they involve fuller recognition that the dreaming consciousness is independent of all physical laws. In such a situation you know, consciously or unconsciously, that you are in an environment that can allow you to take full control of your situation. Also, flying involves you in the exercise of your dreaming intent. You will find that even though you know you can fly, it takes a particular attitude and use of intent to navigate. Flying within dreams enables you to experience the tremendous freedom you have within the Dreamscape, and such dreams usually are accompanied by strong feelings of exhilaration.

Dreaming experiences are unique because individuals are unique. Therefore, you may have yet other types of dreams in which you participate in the process of educating your dreaming focus of consciousness. Certain conditions, however, are consistent throughout. Such dreams always will involve you in some increased understanding about the nature of the Dreamscape and the ways in which your dreaming consciousness functions in that environment. They always will be more than just dreams in which you totally forget who you are and where you are. Just as an increase of understanding within the waking environment generally involves you in stepping back from daily events in order to turn inward and reflect, so does an increase in understanding within the dream environment necessitate a partial detachment from the normal process of dreaming.

Always pay particularly close attention to such dreaming experiences. An assimilation of their lessons from a waking standpoint will increase your ability to understand and interpret your other dreaming experiences. These dreams also will give you a different perspective from which to view all of reality. Recalling such experiences will signal that you have moved beyond the phase of simply remembering your self-created dreaming scenarios and are beginning to recollect some of your experiences from deeper within the Dreamscape.

STUDYING YOUR DREAM LIFE

The myriad aspects of dreaming and the numerous ways in which any explorer of the Dreamscape may go amiss within this dimension makes the interpretation of dreaming experiences a tricky matter. We are bound to make our share of mistakes and false interpretations. If we were so "advanced" that we were not prone to making errors in our investigations, however, we probably would not need to interpret our dreams. To err in investigation is better than not to investigate at all.

As you begin to amass a quantity of recaptured dream experiences there are a few things you can do to make your future explorations and interpretations easier. Begin by noting the similarities in dreams that partake of the same aspects. If, for example, you have discovered a number of dreams with precognitive elements, see if you can discern the unique feeling which accompanies these. Was there a peculiar strangeness to them, or were they particularly vivid? The unique quality of such dreams varies from individual to individual. It is up to you to determine what identifying characteristics are associated with your precognitive experiences. Once you have determined this you will be better prepared to recognize such dreams for what they are when you first recall them, rather than having to wait for their precognitive elements to unfold in your waking life.

Lucid dreams, of course, will be particularly vivid. In your own experience, are they preceded or followed by another specific type of dream? Do they occur only when you have gone to sleep in a particular mood? Are they fully lucid or are there moments when you drift back into fuzziness? Studying these aspects may help you to encourage or initiate more lucid dreams.

In adventure and fantasy dreams you likely will be inclined to engage in adventures that bear obvious similarities to each other. We all choose our own types of adventures; what is challenging to one person may be boring to another. If you know what kinds of adventures or fantasies you typically create you immediately will be able to recognize such dreams for what they are.

You have a particular relationship with every type of experience you have. Challenges or dangers, even as they are encountered in the Dreamscape, will leave a mark upon your psyche, however subtle. Increased understanding through learning-dreams will alter your perspectives on life in a specific way. How you are affected by each type of experience will depend upon your own nature and upon your own relationship with reality. But if you can determine, to whatever degree, how each of these experiences affects you, how it interweaves itself into the fabric of your daily life, then you can not only interpret your dreams more easily, but you also can initiate more effectively the types of experiences which result in the outcomes you want.

Another helpful technique, once you have gained enough familiarity with your dreaming experiences, involves investigating your particular relationship to various symbols. Probably you will find that certain symbols occur again and again in your dreams. They may represent different things at different times, or they may consistently represent the same thing. Whatever the case, it is important to be aware of recurring symbols. Make a list of them and thoroughly examine your associations with them. See if as a group they are somehow connected. Do they all have the same tone? Do they all seem to appeal to the same level of the psyche? Are they private symbols or public symbols?

You also may find that the symbols you employ to represent certain things within your dreams change. At some period in your life you may seem to overhaul your whole symbolic language. Such a process often indicates a comprehensive change in your relationship to and understanding of reality. If this occurs, closely examine how your symbols have changed. Observe the old symbols compared to the new ones. Such an investigation could give you valuable clues as to the nature of the change that has taken place within your own consciousness.

Also, as mentioned before, make note of all "places" to which you travel repeatedly, and of all individuals with whom you repeatedly come in contact within your dreams. Any recurring element, whether person, place, thing, or symbol, is worth investigating thoroughly. The relative continuity of your experiences within the Dreamscape can be better appreciated this way. And, if you are visiting the same place again and again, it is because this place holds some importance for you. Seeing the same people again and again indicates that you have ongoing relationships with them in the Dreamscape. All elements of dreaming have some degree of importance, but recurring elements can give you a better understanding of what is important to you and to your dreaming consciousness.

Consider also the frequency and nature of your dreams as they are related to your state of mind upon going to sleep. Some people find that they recall more dreams when their minds are still racing with thoughts of the events of the day. Others discover that they experience better dream recall when their minds are at peace. Moods, attitudes, states of health, even foods all play a part in determining what kinds and how many dreams you remember.

You may experience increased or diminished dreaming activity at certain seasons of the year. Some people claim that the directional orientation of your bed influences dream recall. Others suggest that temperature and humidity affect the frequency and nature of dreams. The more you can discover about the relationships between your dreams and the other aspects and influences of your life the more effective you will be in exploring and interpreting your dream experiences.

Sharing Dream Experiences with Others

If the opportunity affords itself you may find it helpful to listen to other people recount their dreams. You will necessarily be limited in your ability to interpret their dreams, but if you know a person well you will find it interesting to see how your friend deals with symbols and dream images. Some people have many precognitive dreams and few other types. Some engage in a preponderance of lucid dreams. And some only rarely remember their dreams. In any case, sharing dream experiences can be just as valuable as sharing waking experiences.

If you know others who are involved in exploring the Dreamscape you might attempt shared dreaming. You could agree on a place where you would meet in the dream environment. Or, you might attempt to dream about the same thing. If you have gained some proficiency in lucid dreams or out-of-body experiences you might attempt to contact or call to each other within the Dreamscape. Since it is an objectively valid environment there is no reason why individuals cannot gather together purposefully by conscious intent. You probably won't perceive exactly the same things your friend does even if you do succeed in meeting in the Dreamscape. But the very differences between your experiences could yield much insight.

You also may discover that when you dream about some person you know in waking reality, you are inclined to get in touch with that individual in the physical world. If there is no real barrier to doing so, follow this inclination and see what happens. Often someone you have dreamed about but have not seen for some time will tell you that he or she has been thinking about you. That person may even contact you shortly after your dream experience. (Of course, some people may think you're crazy for getting in touch because of a dream, if you tell them that's what prompted your action.) But doing so will help you find out for yourself just how such dreams tie into your waking reality.

Often dreaming experiences are strange. The interconnections between various levels of consciousness operate in unusual ways. No one can say for certain just what you will discover through an investigation of your own dreams, or through an exploration of the Dreamscape in whatever guise you encounter it. However, you will surely learn something about yourself, and any increase in self-knowledge is valuable. Many people will tell you just what this or that symbol means. All I can say is don't take their word for it. They may be correct in their interpretations of their own personal experiences; their interpretations may even be valid for you, but the only way to be sure is to explore your own relationship to those symbols. It's handy to think that dream interpretation is merely a matter of looking up a symbol in a dictionary, but consciousness and our relationships to reality are not such simple things.

It is, without doubt, a challenge to come to a coherent understanding of the Dreamscape. It takes effort and it takes persistence. There will be disappointing times and there will be encouraging times in your search. There may even be moments when you think that it's all a worthless endeavor. But because we are focused in a reality that has linear time as a parameter, only time will tell just how much you have to gain from such a pursuit.

11

Parting Thoughts for the Pioneering Dreamer

The mass of experience which can be obtained through any exploration of the Dreamscape and our experiences within it is truly overwhelming, and very likely without bounds. In any exploration of ourselves or of any realm of reality, the only limits we have are those resulting from our lack of understanding or ones we have created ourselves. Beliefs and attitudes either can free us for greater discoveries or create boundaries to our possibilities. We must continually reexamine our beliefs in order to determine whether they leave us open to transcending our current concepts or weave a web around us which limits us to our current conceptions. There is always more to learn if we allow ourselves to remain open. The Dreamscape welcomes your approach.

EVIDENCE SUPPORTING THE EXISTENCE OF THE DREAMSCAPE

There is no better place to find conclusive evidence for the reality and validity of the dream environment than in the Dreamscape itself. The more you explore this dimension the more you will find that valuable work occurs there, and that to ignore the experiences encountered there would be to forfeit much. The Dreamscape has its own continuity, its own order, and its own purposes.

Often the seeming lack of continuity of experience within the Dreamscape leads people to deny its objective reality. But this is only an apparent lack, as prolonged investigation shows. As you continue to record your dreams you likely will find, as I have, that while dreaming you have access to the memories of other dreams. Just as in waking reality an event, song, or smell may prompt you to remember something that happened in the past, so in the dreaming environment it is not uncommon to recall one dream while you are involved in another. Such experiences afford evidence that we have a continuity of experience, as well as a real and full life, within the Dreamscape.

Repeated visits to the same locations over the course of our dreaming lives offer further evidence of the continuity of experience within the Dreamscape. Skeptics could maintain that this simply indicates repeated hallucinations or repeated illusionary dreams about the same place. When you experience this phenomenon, however, you will discover that an undeniable feeling accompanies a return visit to a familiar "location." In waking reality you know when you are visiting a place you have been to before; no doubt, a skeptic could label this an illusion as well. Also while dreaming you will know—just as you do in waking life—that you are returning to an old, familiar spot. Each place we visit, whether physically or in dreams, has distinctive feelings associated with it.

Some would claim that the very fact that we do not recall all of our experiences from the Dreamscape is evidence against its reality. But this argument can cut the other way. You will find that while dreaming you recall waking experiences about as well, or as poorly, as you recall dreaming experiences while you are awake. Is this, then, evidence that waking reality is not real? The accuracy and completeness of one's memory is no criterion by which to judge the reality of an event or of a realm—in waking or dreaming life.

Often our strict identification with our experiences within the physical realm leads skeptics to dismiss the dream environment's reality as merely hallucination. The physically oriented aspect of self is trained specifically to function within the physical realm, as we have discussed before, and to operate within the parameters of the physical environment. Its nature involves frequent self-reflection, looking back upon itself to remind itself that it is relatively separate from everything else. This belief in our separateness from all else is a product of our specifically human evolution, but this seeming separateness is not an adequate picture of our true condition. The development of the concept of self as an identity separate from all others and from the environment has been a necessary part of our human evolution; it is a manifestation of the way we, as a species, have chosen to relate to our environment. However, it is not the way our greater consciousness chooses to relate to all environments.

Any gestalt of consciousness quite adequately can retain a sense of identity and inviolable self without always having to say "this is me and that is not me." In the Dreamscape, in particular, our consciousness is secure enough that it can experience reality without always reflecting back on itself. The separate, self-reflecting self is not necessary within the dream environment, nor is it capable of functioning there in the ways to which it has grown accustomed. Self is consciousness; consciousness implies awareness. We are aware within the dream environment whether or not we continually remind ourselves of this.

Some experiences are inhibited by the interjection of the self-reflecting aspect of self. When you are in the process of enjoying a movie to its fullest you often forget who you are so that you can become immersed in the events you are watching. To the degree that you remind yourself you are watching a movie, that you actually are sitting in a theatre seat watching an illusion, you fail to become absorbed in what you are watching and to feel the emotions that are being evoked. In the Dreamscape we often are involved in experiences in which we are meant to let go of rigid notions of self in order to experience self in new ways. If we were to tell ourselves constantly that we are other than what we are experiencing then we would fail to gain all that the experience offers. But in all cases we are still aware, we are still conscious, and we are still inviolable selves. In fact, when we let go of the belief that we are separate, limited selves, we come to discover that we encompass even more than we previously expected.

One of the seeming difficulties in "knowing where we are" while we are dreaming is the result of a natural process. As you go about your daily activities, how often do you remind yourself that you are in the physical realm? The fact is that there is little or no purpose in reminding yourself of the dimension in which you find yourself. We naturally deal with whatever surrounds us; we do not naturally remind ourselves continually that what surrounds us is different from what could be surrounding us. So it is when you are engaged in dreaming; your consciousness does not need to remind itself that it is dreaming.

Nor does it consider its actions as being dreams. It is involved in the reality available at that level of consciousness and it deals with what is at hand.

We attempt to initiate dreams in which we are self-aware in a way with which we are familiar so we can achieve a new leap of consciousness. We are trying to bridge dimensions; we are attempting to experience one dimension from the perspective entertained in another dimension. This new perspective is not necessary; we will continue to function quite adequately in both realms whether we engage in lucid dreams or not. However, we are striving to expand our waking perspective so that it is capable of perceiving and relating to other dimensions of existence. We are trying to evolve beyond the narrow confines of the earth-focused self. No one makes us do this; we do it because expansion of self is inherent in the nature of who and what we are.

We are the determining factor in the nature of our experiences in whatever dimension we find ourselves. This has been said by others, and in a manner far better than I can express. One of the ways we determine our experiences is by choosing to what degree we will participate, here and now, in the infinite experiences of our total consciousness. Denial does not make the Dreamscape any less real; it just closes us off to the experiences encountered therein. Affirmation, on the other hand, opens doors; then we choose when and how we will walk through those doors.

Fear is the greatest obstacle in any exploration of the unknown; it closes doors faster than any affirmation can open them. Fear, under whatever guise and in whatever form, stems from a belief in one's vulnerability to danger. In a universe where we are the architects of our own experiences, a belief in our vulnerability to danger is the only thing that can make us vulnerable to danger.

I feel strongly that we all exist in a state of perpetual grace, that all reality surrounds us with benevolence. I do not believe there is anything "out there" which means to harm us, no devil striving to lead us astray or to tempt us into sin. And I am convinced that there is no punishment for erring. There is, instead, lesson upon lesson in the art of creating our own realities, in self-exploration and self-understanding, and in responsibility. I cannot help but believe that all we do is viewed through the eyes of benevolent grace.

If this is true, then we are safe wherever we travel within the universe. We may undergo periods of disorientation or confusion, but the essence of who we are is indestructible and capable of surviving anything that it experiences. I will not deny that for those who are insecure in their sense of self an intensive exploration of the Dreamscape could lead to psychological problems due to the adjustments that may occur in their sense of self. This would not be the result of malevolent forces, however; rather it would be the result of an individual creating his or her own vulnerability through attitudes of insecurity and fear. Each of us must choose whether to believe that the All nurtures and encourages us, or that we live in a hostile universe.

Preparing for the Future of the Self

It is my belief that inevitably we all will experience focused existence within the Dreamscape or a realm that operates basically the same way. At the moment of physical death we necessarily shed our mortal natures, but this is all physical death is. The self (or soul if you prefer) will continue, but it will continue in a nonphysical state. In that nonphysical realm which we will encounter after the cessation of physical life the parameters and limitations of physical reality will be nonexistent. Linear time will no longer be necessary, nor will the limitations of three-dimensional space. The experiences of all of our incarnations will be available for our viewing. Most likely we will create our own environment, our own reality, instantaneously out of our conceptions and feelings.

None of us knows for certain, of course, whether we will survive beyond physical death. But aside from the testimony which can be gleaned from religious, philosophical, and mystical literature and traditions throughout the ages, there is other evidence to indicate that our consciousness transcends and outlives our mortal forms. In his book *A Practical Guide to Death & Dying,* John White lists eight phenomena which point to the survival of consciousness: evidence of discarnate entities communicating through mediums, apparitions of the dead, out-of-body experiences, memories from past lives, spirit photographs and spirit voice readings, cases of possession, deathbed observations, and near-death experiences.

In particular I would like to discuss out-of-body experiences as evidence for the independence of consciousness from the physical body, since this is the one experience of the eight which nearly everyone can encounter. As White says, citing Dr. Charles Tart, nearly everyone who has an OBE comes away from it with a strong assurance of the survival of the personality beyond physical death. Having an OBE proves to individuals, as much as anything can, that their consciousness can and does operate outside of the confines of the mortal form. This experience, in conjunction with memories from past lives, suggests that consciousness transcends both time and space. According to White, mystics and spiritual teachers traditionally have submitted that time and space are illusions derived from consciousness, indicating that consciousness exists prior to and beyond physical reality.

As mentioned more than once, proof is a subjective thing: what constitutes proof of life after death for one person will not constitute proof for another. Seth, speaking through Jane Roberts, declares that he is a personality who has lived many lives in the physical dimension, and that he is presently an "energy personality essence" existing in nonphysical dimensions. If we cannot accept the evidence for life after death from those now living in physical reality, can we perhaps consider it from those who appear to be focused in nonphysical reality?

If, in the Dreamscape, we can view scenes from our past lives, and if, while there, we are traveling independently of our physical forms, it would be fair to assume that our dreaming experiences are further evidence for the survival of self beyond the point of physical death. And whether we enter the Dreamscape, the nonphysical realms, through dreaming, meditation, or shamanic trance, we are engaging our consciousness as it exists and operates within a nonphysical dimension. We currently have a life within the Dreamscape, we exist and live within nonphysical realms, and there is every reason to believe that we will continue to do so even after physical death.

I believe that the environment we inhabit after physical life operates in a way that is more like the Dreamscape than our waking physical environment, and may indeed be the Dreamscape. For this reason it seems to me that a familiarity with our experiences in the Dreamscape, while we are focused in physical reality, will make the death transition easier. So long as we identify exclusively with the physical form and with the physically oriented self, then the death transition is bound to be somewhat traumatic. But if we explore the nature of our own consciousness and learn now that we exist independently of our mortal form, and if we learn how our experienced reality is unfolded out of our own inner selves, then we will be better prepared for the state of existence to which we will awaken at the moment of physical death.

To become aware of our present existence as a non-physically oriented consciousness, to become aware of our inviolable nature as it exists outside of the bounds of time and space, is to conquer death in the present. If we learn of our past lives now through dreaming, how can we fear extinction at the end of this singular life? If we experience conscious awareness independent of the physical body through dreaming and out-of-body experiences, how can we fear the dissolution of the self with the shedding of the mortal form?

The Dreamscape functions now as a bridge between the inner self and the physically focused consciousness. The inner self has more encompassing purposes and designs than does the earth-self with which we now identify. And obviously it has a more encompassing awareness in regards to the nature of reality, consciousness, and existence. Through the experiences encountered within the Dreamscape the inner self affords the physical self the opportunity to view its life from a wide variety of angles. The inner self allows the physical self to juggle probabilities, to test approaches to life, and to choose which ones to manifest.

It is apparent that the inner self does not interfere

with the choices of the physical self. Though the physical self is part of the inner self, it still has a relatively independent existence. The inner self must gain from the choices and paths of the physical self; it does not simply make the physical self perform in a certain way. We can see that our inner selves manifest portions of themselves in different realms and in different times within the physical realm, but in essence our inner selves set these parts free. As I see it, this is the same as the way in which the All manifests itself in an infinite number of unique gestalts of consciousness, setting them free to experience reality as they choose. Even though the component selves are part of the greater self they are yet inviolable and unique, and their individual experiences contribute to the experience of the whole.

The inner self is always guiding and informing the physically oriented self. Through the Dreamscape, through intuition, and through inspiration it informs the physical self of wider views. Eventually we will partake of the full awareness of our inner selves; we will come to know ourselves as that greater self. But the way in which we grow toward that fuller knowing is through inviting and accepting the guidance of our inner selves. Our inner selves never encourage us to pursue paths that will be unfruitful; they never guide in ways that would be detrimental to our greater fulfillment. But they leave the choice to our conscious awareness as to how and what we will accept and act upon.

There are many people who fear change because they see it as a death of the self. Inevitably change does involve a death of the self. We experience "little deaths" continually; every time we grow we become more than what we were before. Expansion and growth entail the transcendence of what we were before. Growth entails becoming other than, and more than, the selves with which we previously identified. If we all refused to accept change and the accompanying death and transformation, then we would all be children still.

The child often resists "growing up" because it knows that when it is grown it will be different. But we are no longer children. It is time to recognize that we are not static and unchanging. We are not who we were yesterday. Nor will we tomorrow be who we are today. To the degree that we cling to any notion of who and what we are, we limit ourselves and hold ourselves back from becoming more.

Accepting and assimilating the experiences you have within the Dreamscape will necessarily change you. These experiences will change your concept of self, and your concepts regarding the nature of reality. Quite frankly, you will die to yourself, only to be reborn a bit wiser.

If, through examining your dreams, you discover that it is you who has selectively chosen each event which you experience in daily life, then you will be forced to accept a fuller responsibility for everything that "happens to you." If you come to recognize that this life is but a fragment of your total existence and experience, perhaps you will be inclined to take this life less seriously. This doesn't mean you will become frivolous and uncaring about your life; it just means that there might be a little more room in your life for humor, joy, and serenity.

We have no experiences that are devoid of meaning. Everything we experience in our daily lives and in our dreaming lives has value. Whether we choose to experience an event for the fun of it or for the most serious matter of self-expression, it is still important to our overall growth as an ever-expanding gestalt of consciousness. To ignore or to deny any of our experiences is to fail, to some degree, to take advantage of the gift of existence.

Our dreams, whether we recall and interpret them or not, are assimilated as experiences into our total being and thereby contribute to our growth. It is our destiny and responsibility to become increasingly conscious of all that we do, and to become increasingly responsible for all of our actions in all dimensions. At present those experiences which are readily available to our conscious attention are those which we have in our daily lives and those which we undertake within the Dreamscape. We are capable of being conscious of even more experiences, but we first have to accept those of which we are aware now. Dream experiences are there for us to learn from, and if we are to grow as much as it is given for us to grow, we will examine them.

AN INVITATION

It is in the nature of human beings to pioneer new frontiers. We love what is new, unknown, and untried. From the time our earliest ancestors first explored the earth to our present-day journeys into the reaches of space, we have been searching for and exploring new territories. If today there were a newly discovered, uninhabited continent somewhere on earth, many would jump at the chance to go there and test themselves with greater challenges.

We have explored every region of our planet already. We live everywhere, on every continent. There is not a place on the planet that has not been trodden upon, photographed, or flown over. But the earth is but one tiny portion of the infinite reality in which we exist.

The Dreamscape is not, of course, a place to which we can journey physically. But consciousness is not restricted to the confines of physical reality. There are frontiers waiting to be explored; the nature of consciousness and the experiences it has within other dimensions are the frontiers which now call to us. We have explored our physical world; now we must proceed to explore ourselves, our inner worlds, and the other realms to which we have access.

Many have long considered the physically focused self to be the center of their existence. But this self with which we are most familiar rises out of greater sources; it is born into physical existence out of an eternal source. We might look at the physical environment as but a training ground in the art of creation and self-expression. We are called upon to graduate from elementary school and to advance to an understanding of our multidimensional natures.

The Dreamscape is a fertile ground in which to plant the seed of investigation and from which to reap the harvest of heightened awareness. It contains clues to our greater nature and lessons in the art of living. Through the study of our experiences there we may come to live more harmonious and fuller lives in physical reality. At the same time we may extend our horizons to encompass even greater worlds.

Anytime we learn more about ourselves we learn more about the nature of reality. In truth, we can only know reality insofar as we know ourselves. But knowing ourselves requires more than simply exploring our human foibles and our psychological behavior patterns. It requires investigating the ways in which the self we know has come into being. It requires understanding who we are prior to our earth personalities. And it requires letting go of our limited conceptions of the nature of self and the nature of reality.

I do not pretend to know all there is to know about the self or about the Dreamscape. I feel I have just begun to scratch the surface of what can be found in that realm. Neither am I jealous of my discoveries; if anything, I hope others will venture even deeper into the dream environment and tell me what they find. The discoveries of one individual are necessarily limited; each of us must encounter reality through the framework of our own beliefs and through the relative depth of our own understanding. Sharing and comparing is necessary for a more complete view.

The Dreamscape is only one of the frontiers we can enter through the doorway of the self, but it is a valuable one. In the future I hope to be able to share even more of the experiences available to us in this realm. In any event, I intend to continue my explorations. And I truly hope that I soon will hear from some of you as you join the pioneers of this unlimited realm— the Dreamscape.

We publish books on:

Health and Healing ● Eastern Mysticism
Philosophy ● Reincarnation ● Religion
Science ● Transpersonal Psychology
Yoga and Meditation

Other books of possible interest include:

Between Two Worlds by Frederic Wiedemann
Using soul to integrate personality with spiritual nature.

Call to the Heights by Geoffrey Hodson
How to awaken our divine consciousness.

Concentration by Ernest Wood
Meditation using 36 physical and mental exercises.

Devachanic Plane by Charles W. Leadbeater
A clairvoyant description of the "heaven state."

Dreams by Charles W. Leadbeater
What they are and how they are used.

Inner Adventures by E. Lester Smith
Higher thought and how mystics have reached it first.

Inner Life by Charles W. Leadbeater
Study of our unseen nature and that of the universe.

Mastering Your Hidden Self by Serge King
Kahuna awareness of hidden aspects of consciousness.

Psychic Grid by Beatrice Bruteau
How we create the world we know.

The Theatre of the Mind by Henryk Skolimowski
The scope and importance of our evolution.

The Transforming Mind by Laurence and Phoebe Bendit
Our potential for quantum change.

Available from:
The Theosophical Publishing House
P. O. Box 270, Wheaton, Illinois 60189-0270